Archery Today

Archery Today

Techniques and Philosophies in Action

John Kember-Smith

David & Charles

Newton Abbot   London   North Pomfret (Vt)

Dedication

To all the archers I have ever known for their good company
on and off the archery field and for the benefit of all their
thoughts and ideas over the years

British Library Cataloguing in Publication Data

Kember-Smith, John
Archery today : techniques and
philosophies in action.
1. Archery
I. Title
799.3'2   GV1185

ISBN 0-7153-8792-6

Typeset by Typesetters (Birmingham) Ltd,
Smethwick, Warley, West Midlands
and printed in Great Britain
by Butler & Tanner, Frome and London
for David & Charles Publishers plc
Brunel House   Newton Abbot   Devon

Published in the United States of America
by David & Charles Inc
North Pomfret   Vermont 05053   USA

Contents

Foreword

There have been a number of books written about archery, the majority of which have concentrated on a particular aspect of the sport, from introducing the basics up to the more complicated intricacies of preparing equipment for top-class competitive shooting.

Archery Today is different because it covers such a wide range of topics that all archers, whether they are just starting or experienced competitors, will be able to learn from the author's many years of gathering information, which he has now brought together in this book.

There is far more to archery than just shooting a bow and arrow. John Kember-Smith has set out to explain many points which tend to be either overlooked or taken for granted. I am sure that the beginner will appreciate these points, and equally sure that the experienced archer will benefit from refreshing his or her memory about techniques learnt in the past but which have perhaps faded with the passing of time.

I have known the author for very many years, and have a great regard for his enthusiasm and dedication as an archer, which has resulted in him achieving the position of international judge and a much respected coach. So, it is with great pleasure that I recommend this book to archers of all levels who I am sure will benefit from John's many years of experience in the sport.

Dennis Whiteman
President
Grand National Archery Society

CHAPTER ONE

An old, old subject

It is a long time since people in the Western world depended on skill with the bow to put meat in the cooking pot, to defend their homes or attack their enemies – and yet archery still possesses a magical attraction that captures the imagination of the people of today. Their only difficulty is the translation of the idea into some form of practical realisation.

Undoubtedly it is seen by many as a part of the national heritage – bowmen from Britain are remembered on account of the part they played at Agincourt, Crécy and Poitiers – while the legends of Robin Hood, recounted time and time again, still have popular appeal. Many people would love to re-create and maintain some tangible links with such bygone days. Museums, galleries, stately homes and historical literature all play a part in fuelling this desire but individuals rarely get the chance to play an active role.

Shooting in the bow can supply this, being at the same time a modern sport and a positive link with our forefathers and their way of life. The actual holding of a bow in the hand and the shooting of it enables us to partake of a shared experience. Nothing quite compares with the sensation of that first ever arrow successfully sent winging its way to the target.

At its most elementary level, archery is a recreational activity that is in increasing demand in schools and at sports centres up and down the country, limited only by the lack of suitably qualified staff to take charge and by competition for space on sports fields and in sports halls. At the same time it is a highly competitive and demanding sport at all levels right up to and including the Olympic Games.

It is a sport for all ages (almost). Once a young person can stand still for more than a few seconds at a time and has developed a capacity for concentration on the task in hand, archery can be pursued throughout life for just as long as the archer can stand and draw breath.

Everyone knows of people young and old who have never been attracted to taking part in or watching team games (football, hockey, cricket), or individually adversarial games (tennis, squash, boxing) and who feel that they cannot commit themselves to the extent demanded for recognition in individual activity such as swimming or athletics. After eliminating all these, there is still plenty of scope for healthy outdoor recreation, with or without competition – and this is where archery comes into the picture.

Archery opens up a whole new world. Apart from the act of shooting, the skilled archer-craftsman can become bowyer, fletcher or stringer. An internationally recognised Society of Archer-Antiquaries has done and is doing important work in tracing and recording the history of the bow and of the peoples who used it. Other aspects that attract their followings are coaching in the sport and its administration, while it is recorded that one man joined his local archery club because he enjoyed cutting grass – and the club's field and its maintenance was an obvious source of pleasure for him.

Sport for disabled persons is very much a development of the latter part of the twentieth century. For much of the time this is in complete isolation from the able-bodied world, the able-bodied being brought in only as helpers and supporters. Sports where both able-bodied and disabled can compete successfully and on equal terms are almost unheard of – with one very important exception – archery. People working with and on behalf of the disabled are continually pushing back the frontiers so that today it is possible for persons with specific handicaps to take part in archery in a way quite unthinkable twenty years ago.

Internationally archery is a growing sport. Every year more nations are listed among the members of the international archery federation, Fédération Internationale de Tir à l'Arc (FITA) to give a total in 1987 of 70. Figures for the actual numbers of archers are difficult to come by. There are many recreational archers in sports centres and similar places who need never affiliate to their national archery association. In some countries archery may have large numbers of bow hunters who have no connection with organised competitive archery in any form. Elsewhere the adherents of a particular discipline of archery have set up their own group with international links independent of FITA. Thus are the compilers of statistics defeated.

In the United Kingdom there are currently about 15,000 members of the national governing body, the Grand National Archery Society (GNAS), itself a member association of FITA.

One difficulty, common to a number of countries, is that many bodies concerned with sport education and sport promotion have no contact with archery, and hence they ignore it completely. Barriers are slowly being broken down but to archers the process seems to be measured in generations rather than in years. One aim of this book is to build a bridge, providing such organisations with better information on archery as it is today, and thus to pave the way for further development of the sport.

CHAPTER TWO

Laying the foundations

A question often asked by non-archers is 'What is the purpose of archery? Modern man does not use it in warfare, neither does he need it to hunt for essential food.' If the statement which follows the question is true then it becomes necessary to set out the objectives of archery today:

1   To gain pleasure from shooting in the bow
2   To place each separate arrow as close to the mark aimed at as possible
3   To so understand the workings of the body and the bow that the first two objectives are the more easily realised

The first message comes through loud and clear. If no personal satisfaction is derived from an activity then it soon becomes an unpleasant chore, the more so if it is a leisure pursuit for which the individual receives no reward.

As to the second, the ultimate goal is marksmanship of the highest order through the use of the bow. Because of the physical and mental input required, the bow is a primitive machine by comparison with the sophisticated firearms of today, and therein lies the challenge that archery holds for the individual marksman.

Finally, experience has shown that large numbers of archers are lost to the sport every year because they lack the understanding of how best to use their bodies so that they can, in turn, make effective use of the bow.

The artillery comparison

It is no accident that our forebears' use of the word 'artillery' encompassed the bow as well as firearms. The parallel exists today. Taking the fixed coast defence gun as a prime example, the first requirement is a firm platform upon which to mount the weapon so that differences between successive shots are minimised. The archer's equivalent is a firm and unvaried standing position each time he takes his place on the shooting line.

Next comes precise control of traversing and of elevation and depression. It has been said that archery is unlike other sports in that it does not call for the application of any normal human activity such as running, jumping,

The end of a tournament: two archers who have thoroughly enjoyed themselves

throwing, kicking or striking with or without any kind of stick as an aid. Wrong; the archer points – not just with his finger or arm – but with his whole body where arm and fingers are extensions of the body, moving with it and not independently. In traversing to bring the fall of shot from the side to centre on the target, the whole body is moved by a shift of foot position, perhaps almost undetected – by a few millimetres for fine adjustment – perhaps by several centimetres, to set up the initial shooting position. The gunnery parallel has a pivot, about which the mounting turns, and a carriage with wheels or bearings to take the weight and allow free movement about the pivot with machinery enabling rapid adjustment and fine control.

Elevation to increase the range or to place the shot higher in the target area, and depression to decrease the range and place the shot lower, is achieved at a single pivot, normally at a point on the axis of the gun barrel so that the mass of the barrel is balanced by the mass of the breech and recoil mechanism. The gun barrel is matched in archery by the relationship of the upper part of the body, neck, head and arms. In holding the drawn bow the relative alignment of these components must be constant otherwise the archer will be bending the gun barrel. With a firearm a bent barrel leads to a disastrous explosion, damaging to friend instead of foe. In archery the damage is not to fellow archers but to the archer's own performance.

The pivot for elevation or depression cannot therefore be at wrist, elbow, shoulder or neck, so what remains that is capable of being controlled? Physiologically the area of the archer's hips is the ideal pivot, the legs and pelvis being his equivalent of the carriage on which the gun barrel is pivoted. He uses the flexibility of the lower part of the spine to produce the desired amount of movement − slight compared with the range through which the archer could move.

A measured amount of powder as the propellant charge for the gun will give a predictable muzzle velocity using standard projectiles. The artillery-man will know that if he uses a standard charge with a standard projectile his range will be known within predictable limits for a given elevation. Adjustment to bring the shot on target depends upon observation of the fall of shot. For an archer the arrows he uses are identical in weight, stiffness, length and fletching; for him they are standard projectiles. However, though a bow is identified as having a specific draw weight when drawn through a given length and will therefore give predictable results when mounted in a shooting machine, in the hands of an archer it is subject to many variables due solely to the human agency.

The drawing of the bow supplies the means by which the arrow is propelled − the further the bow is drawn the greater the amount of propellant energy stored to await the release. The objective of the archer is to develop bodily control in drawing the bow to standardise as nearly as possible the amount of propellant energy available for each shot he makes.

In other words, he draws or should draw the string back to his face by precisely the same amount for every arrow shot, and likewise he releases the string in exactly the same way in every shot that he makes. This degree of precision is difficult to achieve but there are archers today who closely approach this ideal while many more could do so were they to have enough practice.

That is why 'possible' scores are known only in certain short range indoor archery contests, and why even in the Olympic Games and the World Target Archery Championships the very best scores are about 200 points short of the maximum 2,880.

What any archer, coach or coached, seeks to do is to minimise the effects of these variables. There are other sources of variation due to equipment and environment, but the important ones in archery will always be the physiological and psychological factors − things completely foreign to the gunner.

The archer as an athlete
So far the composite image of the archer using the bow has been likened to a piece of artillery. But the archer himself is also an athlete, even though many practising archers would deny this. The dictionary defines an athlete as 'a

competitor or skilled performer in physical exercises; robust or vigorous person'. Competitor an archer certainly is – he competes not only against standards set by fellow competitors but also against any he has set previously for himself. The archer is also a skilled performer, a solo performer whenever he takes his place on the shooting line. His performance depends in no way upon those of the other archers on the line. Moreover, to look good and to produce an acceptable score the archer must develop a high degree of skill so as to control body and bow with the degree of precision that good shooting requires.

'Robust' as applied to an archer does not mean sheer physical strength and massive muscle but more of an inner strength, capable of withstanding the environmental and mental pressures encountered in the course of a day's shooting. Similarly 'vigorous' (strong and active) refers again not only to the ability to draw the bow but also to the inner strength to exercise effective control of it while being mentally active to sense all the factors immediately affecting the shot he is about to make.

If an archer shoots 150 arrows in the course of a day's shooting he will have drawn his bow at least that number of times. If his bow has a draw weight of 40lb (draw weights of bows are always given in pounds without metric equivalents) for his arrow length, then he will have taken that load across his shoulders no less than 150 times giving an accumulated total of 6,000lb or approximately 2¾ tons. At the same time, in an event shot under international rules, he will have walked nearly 4.5km (2.8 miles) just from waiting line to target and back again.

It will be seen that archery is an activity that does not call for sudden explosive bursts of energy but for sustained and controlled application of effort, both in competition and in preparatory training.

The image of archery

Those not connected with archery have varied ideas concerning its nature, mostly related to the past. Robin Hood legends have been perpetuated on cinema and television screens in the context of which the layman thinks of medieval revival and expects participants to wear fancy dress costume of Lincoln Green and to shoot with longbows. Classical scholars may well have mental pictures of the heroes of the Trojan War. Childhood fantasies of the 'Wild West' in countless games of 'cowboys and injuns' colour a further vision while an image exists of Victorian gentility and passion for long, obscure words where more simple and effective words exist – why else would 'toxophily' appear as a symbol of their erudition?

The common bond for all these non-archers is that few know that archery today is actively pursued throughout the world as an Olympic sport with an increasing and welcome participation of 'third world' nations. Nevertheless these laymen express a desire to have experience of archery, however fleeting.

14

Safety

One image of archery is common to elected representatives from Members of Parliament down through county, district and town councillors. Their collective lack of knowledge of archery is summed up in the one word 'dangerous'. Their lack of knowledge is indeed dangerous for archery, so an examination of the facts would not go amiss.

In the United Kingdom the provision of playing fields, parks and open spaces is centred around the traditional games of cricket and football or for the enjoyment of open space within the towns. Dedicated archery ranges, whether for community or club use or large enough for major tournaments, do not exist, although some enterprising clubs have secured exclusive tenure of land for archery while a few actually own their own shooting grounds.

Consequently much archery today is an open-field activity, taking place on fields shared with other sports. When archery is taking place football or cricket pitches may be unusable and when football or cricket are being played archery is out of the question (see overleaf). In the event of a conflict of interest archery lacks support from non-archers.

Of necessity archery has had to adopt a range discipline appropriate to open-field use. No matter what the scale, from small club to major event, whenever shooting takes place one person is appointed as field captain. It is his duty to give the signal to start shooting; to signal, when all archers have shot their arrows, that they should advance to score and collect them and – most important – to stop shooting immediately in an emergency or possible hazard. In addition, any archer who sees a hazardous situation arising may himself signal for shooting to stop at once by giving the traditional call *'fast!'*.

As to accidents in archery, since World War II there has been only one recorded occasion in archery organised under the auspices of the GNAS when a person has been injured by another's arrow.

On grounds where the public has access the GNAS rules of shooting are quite specific on the question of laying out the archery range and where the boundary rope should be located to keep the public out of harm's way.

The same rules of shooting lay down that a bow may not be drawn except on the shooting line and in the direction of the target. FITA rules are even more specific: 'No archer may draw his bow, with or without an arrow, except when standing on the shooting line. If an arrow is used, the archer shall aim towards the targets but only after being satisfied that the range is clear both in front of and behind the targets.'

One thing ought to be immediately obvious; no archer can say of his bow 'I did not know it was loaded'.

Finding archery and archers

Communications vary from nation to nation as do their systems. Even within

15

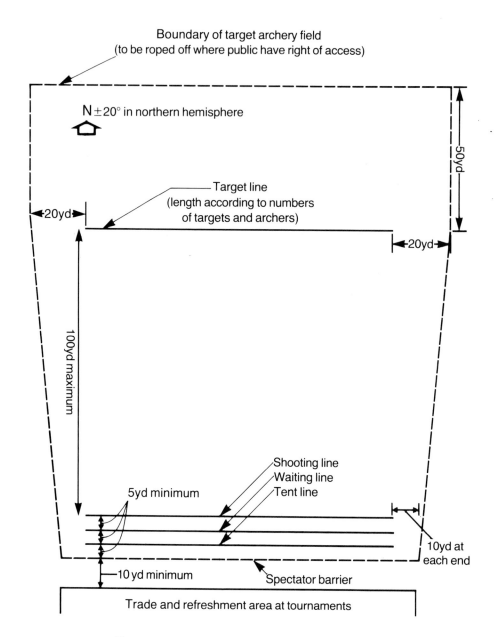

Boundary of target archery field
(to be roped off where public have right of access)

N ±20° in northern hemisphere

Target line
(length according to numbers
of targets and archers)

50yd

20yd

20yd

100yd maximum

Shooting line
Waiting line
Tent line

5yd minimum

10yd at
each end

10 yd minimum

Spectator barrier

Trade and refreshment area at tournaments

Target archery field layout (GNAS Rules)

one country there may be numerous separate agencies dealing with archery; one department may know exactly how and where to contact the sport, while another remains completely at a loss.

The interested layman wants to know where he can find archery and get in touch with archers. The best advice is to start with local sources of information. Public libraries or sport and leisure administrations make good starting points while newspaper offices can be sources of even the most unlikely information. Sadly, local directories and guidebooks are not much help largely because most archers are reticent individuals, shunning publicity and doing their own thing in semi-privacy.

Only when all possible local sources have been found wanting should it be necessary to extend the search. Here umbrella sports associations covering a whole region may supply the answer or, as in at least one European country, there may be a single organisation embracing all projectile sports. At national level there will be the national governing body (about seventy of them around the world) or, should it prove difficult to track down, the national Olympic committee or a national newspaper could point the enquirer in the right direction.

So, if you want to find out more about archery in your part of the world, never take 'no' for an answer. Persist until contact has been made – your efforts will be well rewarded.

CHAPTER THREE

Clothing and equipment for beginners

Almost everyone knows what the preferred or obligatory clothing is for tennis, cricket, athletics, squash, badminton or football. Few people would tackle any of these activities without being properly clothed.

In archery the beginner is at a loss as to what should be worn for comfort and effectiveness. Even his mentors in club or leisure centre are not as forthcoming on this topic as they might be. Archery coaches are often heard to say that coaching begins with the feet and works upwards. With clothing, too, this is the best way.

Shoes

The importance of footwear in archery tends to be overlooked so let it be emphasised how essential it is to have the right kind of covering for the feet. In a target archery event the archer spends much of his time standing on the shooting line and walking to and from the target. In field archery the competitors are continually on the move from target to target, and – as with target archery – most events are whole day affairs.

For men and women alike a firm and stable foundation is the prime requirement; the gun mounting of the previous chapter. The needs of archery have nothing to do with current fashion so it must be accepted that good archery footwear will be somewhat unfashionable. The area of contact of sole and heel with the ground must be as large as possible, especially at the heel.

Women will be very well aware that small heels sink into soft ground. Heel height can be critical – body weight must not be thrown forward. At the same time, since most people wear shoes with heels in their everyday activities it is sensible to have shoes with some sort of heel – ¾ to 1in (2 to 2½cm) would be about right – otherwise not only does the balance not feel right but substantial discomfort could be felt by the end of the day.

Archery today is an all-weather sport, halted only by the most extreme conditions. Perhaps it is asking the impossible in saying that shoes for archery should be cool when the weather is hot and warm when the temperature has fallen substantially, and waterproof at all times. Nevertheless it is worthwhile to try and meet these requirements as nearly as possible.

All these things will be of no account if the shoes are not comfortable and here lace-up shoes will have the advantage over those that just slip on. It makes good sense for the archer to keep one pair of shoes set aside solely for wear on the archery field.

Socks of natural fibre are comfortable and help the feet to breathe and so moderate the effects of heat and cold.

Field archery, conducted over uneven terrain, calls for sterner measures. The going can be very rough so there is nothing to beat a stout pair of walking boots, well broken in, which give that much needed support for the ankles while possessing all the other qualities required in target archery.

Choice of clothing

Clothing presents some problems, for it is difficult to devise a formula for worldwide application. Climate varies not only from country to country but also within a country. Some parts of the world experience unpredictable variations in weather. It is perhaps better to look at the needs of such countries and leave those more fortunate to look after themselves.

It is important that no part of any clothing should be in the path of the bowstring at any time. This means that all garments should fit snugly around the arms and upper part of the body with no folds, buttons or trimming that might be touched by the bowstring. In changeable weather, several easily removable light layers are better then a single heavyweight item. At the same time the garments, singly and combined, should permit total freedom of movement of the arms and shoulders.

Waterproofing is the worst problem of the lot. Waterproof clothing is notoriously bulky, while one can get as wet inside as out from perspiration that would normally evaporate unnoticed. The beginner does not have to worry about this just yet – his training would not continue in the rain – but it is a point to consider when he develops into a competitive archer and he should be aware of what the future will require of him.

Headgear

Headgear is a matter of individual choice. In cold weather a hat will supplement the natural insulation provided by the hair. Under a cloudless sky the same hat or cap will help to prevent sunburn while the peak or brim reduces glare. The most important consideration is that peak or brim should obstruct neither the bowstring nor the archer's vision.

Looking after the hands

Cold hands are enemies of good shooting. Training sessions for beginners may coincide with unseasonable cold weather. Fingerless gloves give protection to the wrists and backs of the hands where blood vessels are close to the surface and not only help to keep the hands warm and conserve body heat but also permit free movement of the fingers. It should go without saying that when not shooting extra layers can be added wherever needed; a cold archer will not give of his best.

Colour

The beginner might well ask about suitable colours for archery clothing. This is not immediately important, although most nations have dress regulations applicable to the more renowned events in their calendars. When in doubt it is enough to consider the archer as an athlete and to say 'all white is all right'.

Bows for beginners

Equipment for beginners varies enormously according to who provides for their training. In schools and leisure centres equipment is pooled and used by all comers. It therefore has to be as nearly indestructible as possible and capable of withstanding any amount of careless handling. Here the solid fibreglass bow will be the mainstay, despite its acknowledged drawbacks. While these are not so serious with persons of average size, they create problems with people of well above average height and build. First, the overall length of the bow will be such that the string makes a more acute angle with the arrow when the bow is fully drawn with a suitably long arrow and thus compresses the fingers to a greater extent; the fingers in such a case are likely to be larger than average anyway. Then the handle shape and size will be incompatible with the larger hands of the outsize novice.

The pools of equipment in these places have to be available for a wide variety of age groups while provision of equipment is subject to strict budgetary control. The inevitable result must be a compromise, with the initial training of the beginner done with bows that are possibly a little too heavy (typically about 25–30lb for adults) so that once they have ceased to be absolute beginners a reasonable standard of performance is possible with the same bows. Sadly, this does not always work out.

Ideally a start should be made with lighter bows (say 15lb) so that correct posture and control can be easily learned before refining shooting technique and then graduating to bows with draw weights nearer to those used in competition (in the range from 25lb upwards to about 35lb for adults while they are consolidating their earlier work). A person who chooses, in spite of all advice, to shoot with an excessively heavy bow too early in his initiation into archery is not a hero, but merely an idiot.

In the case of young people the issue is complicated by their varying growth rates and differing sizes and strengths for a given age, apart from the inability of many children to appreciate what they are required to do with their bodies in order to develop a recognisable shooting form. The simple fibreglass bows, best suited to young people who have not yet entered their

A simple fibreglass bow suitable for equipment pools. It rests on an inexpensive ground quiver

teens, tend to be lacking in power, with high arrow trajectories and arrows that often rebound from the target.

In many clubs and wealthier institutions beginners can start with bows of composite construction (where the working parts of the bow consist of laminations of fibreglass on a wooden core). Here tuition would be given on a one-to-one basis or to very small groups so that the risk of mishandling or accidental damage to the bow is greatly reduced. It would be foolish, and costly, to use composite bows as pooled equipment in schools or sports centres.

Take-down bows have the advantage that the same handle section can be fitted with limbs of progressively greater draw weight to match the new

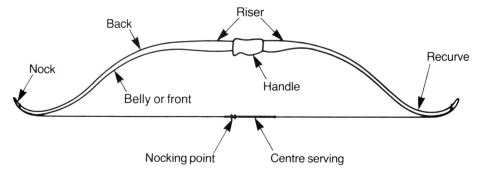

The parts of a simple one-piece bow

Specialist archery retailers often attend major tournaments: a selection of take-down bows on display

archer's settling down into a consistent and effective way of shooting. Similarly, longer limbs offering the same effective draw weight can keep up with a young archer's rate of growth. Alternatively, and probably better, the original limbs can be fitted to a longer handle.

Caution is needed here – each manufacturer uses a different system of fitting the limbs to the handle, while the system used for current models may differ from that used for earlier ones. Regrettably there are no national or international standards for the methods of fitting limbs to the handle sections of take-down bows. This may be fine for the manufacturers and dealers and for their profit margins, but it is of no help to their customers who may be compelled to spend far more than should be necessary.

What is needed, perhaps, is for independent bowyers to specialise in the manufacture of limbs with fittings adaptable to any common make of handle and that can be sold at prices attractive to the customer.

Bowstrings

Bowstrings made from Dacron are best suited for beginners' bows. They should have sufficient strands in their make-up so that, served with normal soft twist nylon thread, they fit snugly into the nocks of the arrows, being neither so thick that they have to be forced into the nocks, nor so thin that the arrows fall off. Twelve strands of Dacron are just right for most arrow nocks and the nocking point does not then have to be built up specially. Some authorities quote varying numbers of strands according to the draw weight of the bow but for the new archer (and for the majority of established archers, too) this is an unnecessary refinement.

For fibreglass training bows for adults a bracing height of 8in (20cm) is about right, with somewhat less for the smaller bows of the younger beginners. With bows of composite construction the manufacturer's recommended bracing height should be strictly adhered to. If a range is quoted, such as 9½–10½in (23.75–26.25cm), the midpoint of the range is certainly the best for shared use or as a starting point for a beginner's first purchase.

Arrows

Arrows for beginners' use are now made from aluminium alloy. Wood is to be avoided though it has its uses in field archery. A first requirement is that they should be robust since they are communal property and subject to a lot

Arrows
Top: *school arrows with insert nocks, conical piles and feather fletchings*
Centre: *more robust beginners' arrows with fit-on nocks, steel bullet piles and plastic vanes*
Bottom: *British-made competition arrows*

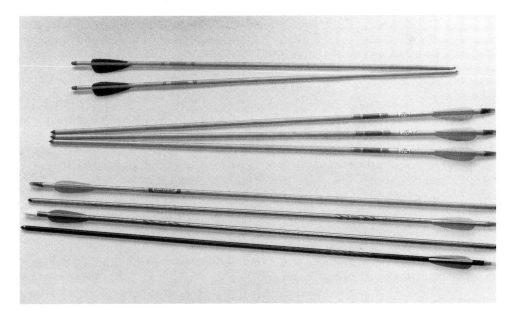

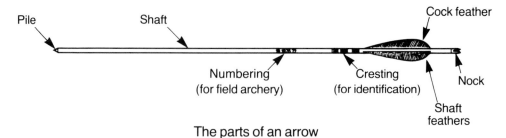

Pile   Shaft   Cock feather

Numbering
(for field archery)

Cresting
(for identification)

Nock

Shaft
feathers

The parts of an arrow

of ill-treatment. The alloy arrows sold as school or beginners' arrows have proved their worth in such circumstances, especially when fitted with flexible plastics vanes instead of natural feathers. They withstand much mishandling and, when they become bent, can be straightened with comparative ease again and again before they reach breaking point through metal fatigue. Many have hard aluminium alloy conical piles and insert nocks, again easily replaced in case of damage.

Traditional fletchings for arrows are made from natural feathers, and these are still used for many of the arrows supplied for school or beginners' use. These suffer from repeated use out of doors in all weathers and flexible plastics vanes, universally used today for serious competition in both target and field archery, have proved better able to withstand the rough usage of a school environment.

While experienced archers often have all the fletchings on their arrows of the same colour it is more traditional – and more useful for the novice – to have the cock feather (the one at right angles to the slot in the nock of the arrow) of a different colour as a visual reminder that the arrow should always be placed on the string with the cock feather standing away from the bow.

The packages in which school and beginners' arrows are supplied are not robust or suited for communal use where they soon disintegrate. Homemade wooden racks are far better for withstanding wear and tear, or an equipment case for personal use.

A suitable length of arrow for an individual can only be decided by a coach. Until the new archer has settled into a consistent way of shooting (a process that may take several weeks depending upon personal response to instruction), it is imperative that arrows longer than necessary are used to provide a margin of safety against the arrow being drawn inside the bow should the archer hyperextend himself. Even when the new archer has settled into a controlled shooting technique it still pays to have a slightly greater arrow length than necessary for a time – he may extend himself more as the back and shoulder muscles gain strength through repeated use. A long arrow can always be made shorter but short arrows need replacement by longer ones, and it is the archer who will pay if by this time he has already bought his own.

Arrows for use in schools and leisure centres have to be available in several lengths to suit those taking part; but a strict watch must be kept on allocation of arrows to students so that an archer who should use 30in arrows rather than 26 or 28in shafts actually does so.

In archery clubs the training equipment will often include arrows handed down by members who regularly replace their own personal equipment and these will be of better quality than those purchased for school use. Such arrows are often loaned to new recruits for longer periods, so that the behaviour of different specifications of arrow shot with their own personal bows can be assessed before they set out to buy arrows for themselves.

Accessories

The first purchases of a new archer are likely to be tab and bracer. A shooting tab is as personal to an archer as an item of clothing. It can be trimmed to suit the length and breadth of the archer's fingers and with use will acquire that degree of suppleness that no brand new tab will ever possess. Shooting off the bare fingers with a light bow has its advantages during initial training but as the number of arrows shot in each training session increases the fingers feel the strain. Apart from this the smoothness of the skin varies from day to day, depending upon humidity. The use of the tab with its consistently

Simple tab and bracer suitable for beginners

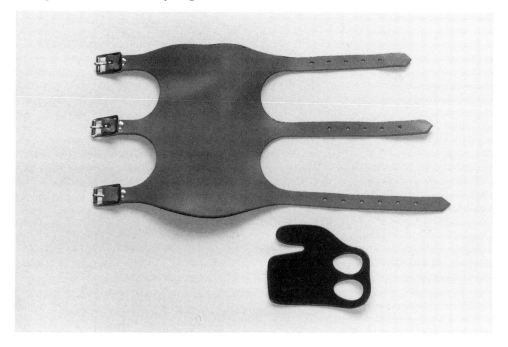

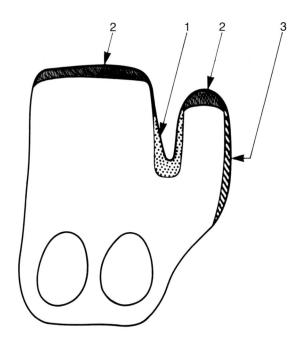

1 Trim if too narrow or shallow
2 Trim if too long
3 Trim if it affects hand location

A basic shooting tab

smooth surface overcomes this and introduces a welcome uniformity into the way in which the string leaves the fingers. Some new archers say that they cannot get used to the tab. This is only because first of all it has to be trimmed to suit the archer's fingers – remembering all the time that it is always possible to cut off a little bit more but quite impossible to stick anything back on – and then it has to be broken in so that it loses its initial rigidity.

The bracer or armguard has as its main function that of keeping the folds of the sleeve of shirt or sweater out of the path of the bowstring. It is worn on the inside of the forearm and held in place with straps, which should hold the bracer firmly so that it does not slip but at the same time does not impede circulation. The bracer also offers protection to the arm should the string strike it (if this happens repeatedly it should remind the archer that he has allowed his technique to break down).

The next item on the shopping list is a quiver for the arrows. It is far more efficient to take an arrow from a belt quiver than to pick one up from the ground. Energy is not wasted in the bending or stretching that would otherwise be necessary. Quivers can be quite elaborate in their styling and trims but otherwise offer no advantage over more basic models. Those in manmade materials are cheaper than those of leather but are well designed and robust. Budget-conscious beginners will do well to compare the prices of locally made items with imported equivalents.

Arrows do not always hit the target. A wool tassel suspended from the archer's belt is a useful accessory for removing soil from arrows that have landed in the ground. They can be purchased from archery shops. Alternatively they can be made at home in colours to the archer's choice.

A bow stand for use indoors or out is more of a luxury in an initially tight budget but is nevertheless a sound investment.

The bow sight

This item has deliberately been left as the last on the list. Not that it is unimportant – rather that its importance is often over-rated and emphasised far too early in the life of a new archer. It is simply a device that the archer will place on the line of sight when drawing his bow so that, all other things being equal, he will elevate the bow by the same amount for every shot that he attempts.

It is used in target and free style field archery because it offers greater precision than can be obtained through using the point of the arrow as an aid to aiming (see overleaf).

Pooled equipment is treated with such scant respect that anything like a competition bow sight can never be justified, apart from the problems of fixing such devices to fibreglass bows. A strip of self-adhesive fabric tape or foam draught excluder stuck to the back of the bow, into which a glass-headed dressmaker's pin can be inserted, makes a simple and effective bow sight for the beginner that can be quickly replaced if damaged.

Bow sights for personal use, no matter how simple or complex, conform to the following basic pattern: some form of track on which the sight attachment can slide up and down and a means of locking the attachment in the desired position. In the sight attachment there is a screw-threaded device for lateral adjustment. The actual sight may be in the form of a bead, crosswires, aperture or interrupted crosswires.

The purchaser should make certain that whatever bow sight he buys will fit securely on his bow – some are better suited to mounting on a curved surface than others. Even simple bow sights are vulnerable to accidental knocks so it is an advantage if the sight attachment or – even better – the whole sight track can be removed from the bow and kept safely when not in use.

27

(left) *Simple bow sight for pooled use, using draught excluder under fabric tape and a glass-headed dressmaker's pin*

(right) *Simple commercial bow sight suitable for the first-purchase or Standard bow*

Buying that first bow

New or secondhand, the beginner's first bow will be an exciting landmark in his career. No subsequent purchase will ever generate such a thrill.

If he heeds the advice given by the coaches he will become the possessor of a bow suited to his physique and to his immediate capabilities with a sensible margin for development. The draw weight will not be as great as that which might later prove most useful, but it is important that it is something the archer can control rather than something that dominates the archer. This means that the best performance will be at intermediate rather than at the maximum target archery distances.

The archer must avoid heroics – never mind what the veterans might do to encourage shooting at greater distances with heavier bows. Too many archers are lost to the sport because they began with bows well beyond their control and have soon lost what shooting form they had. The ensuing disheartenment takes them out of archery, the more so if they are reluctant to admit that they tried to do too much too soon.

There is no hard and fast formula to determine what bow will suit which person. If only it were that easy! All that can be done is to offer a framework that should ensure no serious errors occur. The table in Appendix 2 supplies this.

Buying the first arrows

Which comes first, the bow or the arrows? If the archer is likely to be using a bow from the equipment pool for a long time and is also using pool arrows it might be wise to buy a relatively inexpensive set of arrows, which he can truly call his own.

Once he has his own bow the situation is quite different. Arrows that do not match the bow will not form tight groups at the target, no matter how good the archer's shooting form might be. The starting point will be the manufacturers' selection charts. These charts give, for a combination of draw weights and arrow lengths, the optimum shaft diameter and wall thickness of the tubing that should allow the arrow to leave the bow cleanly.

If allowance is to be made for anticipated growth, or for development of shooting form, then the actual arrow length must be greater than the effective draw length and both lengths must be considered when using the charts. For example, where the effective draw length is currently 25in and development of shooting form is likely, an actual length of 26in could be appropriate.

Another factor is important for archers who have not developed to the point where they can guarantee to place their arrows on the target at the short and intermediate ranges – arrows that are destined to hit the ground or the legs of the target stands fairly frequently need to be not only robust but capable of being straightened without developing kinks in the tube walls. Here it would be wise to select shafts with the smallest available diameter and the thickest walls within the limits set by draw length and draw weight. The net result will be arrows that may be heavier and therefore need more elevation for shooting at a given distance.

Arrow shafts are now specified by outside diameter in units of $\frac{1}{64}$in and by wall thickness in units of $\frac{1}{1000}$in while length is measured from the shoulder of the pile to the bottom of the nock. The effective draw length is from where the arrow makes contact with the arrow rest to the bottom of the nock.

An arrow quoted as 1816 will have an outside diameter of $\frac{18}{64}$in and a wall thickness of $\frac{16}{1000}$in. In the course of conversation archers will talk about these numbers quite happily, leaving the layman wondering what they mean.

The trend among competitive archers is towards using larger diameter shafts with thin walls to keep arrow weight down and thus have faster arrows with a flatter trajectory. But of course they expect to hit the target every time.

Bits and pieces

With successive purchases the archer will amass a collection of items that he will have to carry around whenever he goes to club or tournament. A one-piece bow needs its own bag and a separate container for arrows and accessories. With take-down models even a relatively inexpensive tackle case will hold everything – bow, arrows and accessories. The archer's task will be to go through his tackle case regularly to weed out unwanted items that accumulate. A well ordered tackle case is the hallmark of a good archer.

General advice

It is sad that the consumer is so often dazzled by brand names and by the image of conspicuous consumption. This relates to archery equipment just as much as to other commodities.

However, it makes sense to consider locally made products rather than the imported wherever possible. It is often cheaper and also more readily available while of a quality more appropriate to local conditions.

It makes good sense to keep the equipment simple in the early stages. The archer has enough to do in developing his shooting form without introducing unnecessary and often expensive complexities. He will find that in applying himself to developing control of his bow he will not need to complicate matters by imitating others. In the club the new member will find that he will be swamped by lots of conflicting, though well intentioned, advice, often at variance with what his coach is seeking to achieve. Be interested and listen by all means, but please discuss it with your coach before attempting to put it into practice.

The recent history of archery equipment has produced many items introduced to compensate for human frailty and that have since been adopted almost universally by many who do not need such things, rather like an able-bodied person who persists in using crutches as an aid to walking.

CHAPTER FOUR

Shooting Technique

Roger Ascham (1515–1568), in his book *Toxophilus*, set out his ideal of good shooting in five parts; standing, nocking, drawing, holding and loosing. Today's approach to shooting technique still embraces them though the emphasis has changed as knowledge of the human body has developed, and as the shortcomings of countless thousands of archers have been analysed and discussed by generations of coaches. It would be a rash person who maintains even now that the last word has been said.

Most people coming into archery wish to discover what it is like to shoot in a bow. They expect to shoot within minutes of introduction to the bow, not realising that to shoot properly calls for a lot of input from both coach and pupil. The coach may lose pupils if he is too long-winded in the beginning so he may allow a 'taster' in which they shoot a dozen or so arrows with a minimum of preliminary detail. After that he will better be able to get down to the real business of teaching them to control both body and bow.

It is not possible to give any equivalent of the 'taster' in print because so many things will remain unexplained. Hence the framework set out by Roger Ascham all those years ago will be expanded and brought up to date in the following pages.

One necessary preliminary to instructing a beginner, something not taken into account by Ascham, is to discover whether the pupil is left- or right-handed. Most right-handed persons will find it easier to hold the bow in the left hand and place the fingers of the right hand on the string, while those who are left-handed will find it more natural to take the bow in the right hand.

When this has been taken care of there may still be a problem remaining for some people, that of 'eye dominance' or preference for using one eye rather than the other in a task where only one eye is required to do the work; for example when using any optical instrument with only a single eyepiece. Much used to be made of eye dominance but today it is dealt with only when it is seen to interfere with the individual's mastery of the bow.

Knowledge of whether the pupil has left or right eye dominance is useful background knowledge and this is the time to test the new archers for this. The procedure that is most practical, not involving any equipment, is for the coach to stand about 5m (5½yd) away from his pupil, cover one eye with his hand and then ask the pupil to point his index finger at the uncovered eye, first with one hand and then with the other while keeping both eyes open. In the majority of cases the finger will line up with the pupil's dominant eye and so the coach will have a clear cut idea of how he should proceed.

When the result is not clear cut, it usually means that there is no marked eye dominance. Here the archer must remember which eye to use when aiming and must drill himself in this so that he does not run into difficulties later.

Various authorities have suggested that about one third of all right-handed persons have left eye dominance while about half of all left-handed persons have right eye dominance. In archery the archer holding the bow in his left hand is expected to aim with the right eye to obtain the greatest control over the accuracy of his shooting and with the left eye if the bow is held in the right hand.

It is not wise to ask the archer with a dominant left eye to close it if he should be using the right one. This may prove to be physically impossible and even if not, the resulting facial tension is uncomfortable and does not promote good shooting. The real and immediate answer is to ask the archer to use a patch to cover the eye and thus free the facial muscles from strain.

Pupil with dominant right eye as seen by the coach

Once regarded as 'cissy', patches are now much more widely used by those who need them.

This still leaves some right-handed archers whose vision from the right eye is impaired so that it cannot be used for aiming. If this is the case, it is best to transfer the bow to the other hand. Since archery is a new and untried activity this should not present any serious problem, although it may slow down the rate of learning the necessary skills. There are other solutions but in most cases they create as many problems as they solve.

Standing

This gives a firm platform from which all good shooting follows. The essentials are comfort and stability. If an archer is not comfortable he will not shoot well because his mind will be on his discomfort rather than on the job in hand. So what is a comfortable position? The starting point for any newcomer is to stand astride the shooting line with the bow hand nearest to the target so that the heels are separated by approximately the width of the shoulders (not shoulders plus upper arms) and the toes very slightly turned out. If the feet are too far apart, tension will be felt around the hips and this causes fatigue. If the feet are too close together there will be a feeling of instability, the more so if a strong wind is blowing.

Standing astride the shooting line is not enough on its own for the archer could be facing almost anywhere. The line through the shoulders should point directly at the target, so for a beginning it is assumed that a line through the heels would do the same. Corrections to take account of individual asymmetry would follow later.

So far only the feet have been considered; what about the rest of the body? Very few people are called upon to stand erect for hours at a stretch in their normal or domestic situations. Most have to direct their attention downwards over workbench, keyboard, kitchen sink or office desk. If the attention is directed downwards the head will follow as will the shoulders. The hands are stretched forward and so are the shoulders with the result that the breathing is shallow and the oxygen intake is minimal. This is no good for any kind of sport.

The archer has to learn how to counteract this and archery coaches, having found that few archers, new or established, really know how to stand erect, have to teach them to develop good posture so that they can properly control their bows.

Tall people are the worst offenders in this respect. Either they are self conscious about their height, especially if they are young and still at school or college, or they are so used to addressing people shorter than themselves that they automatically direct their attention downwards even when they think they are standing erect.

In a class situation the coach can only tell his pupils to 'stand tall', to

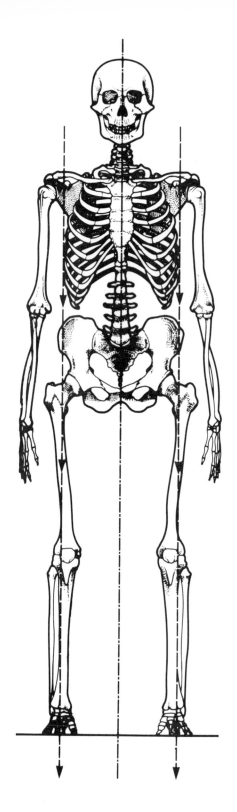

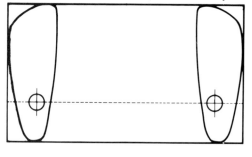

An ideal all round position with minimum loading on joints and minimum muscular tension combined with optimum stability

The structure of standing

stretch themselves, to tuck their tails and tummies in and to look at a point on the horizon or at its indoor equivalent, an identifiable point at eye level, and then in whatever time he can spare quickly to try and deal with the worst cases. There is a tendency at this stage for the head to be slightly tilted back with the chin jutting forward. This can be corrected by gently pulling the chin in; this should be a natural rather than a forced action. Where the coach is working with a single pupil he can spend more time at this stage with greater effect.

When people are asked to stand up straight they adopt a tense and rigid posture, imitating a soldier standing at attention. The coach has to counteract this if he cannot prevent it, and one of the best ways is to work on the pupils' breathing to ease the tension. If the pupils take a series of deep breaths, pushing the air down into the diaphragm, and then exhaling so that the lungs are completely emptied, they will feel the tensions gradually disappear with the exhalations so that they are left standing erect but in a relaxed manner. It is useless to tell people to relax – they just do not know how.

Nocking

In its specific and traditional meaning this is the act of placing the arrow on the bowstring. Today it is just one of several parts of the preparation for making the shot.

Preparation is important. An inadequately prepared shot will not be a good one. Preparation includes:

1 establishing a good hold on the bow;
2 placing the arrow on the string;
3 placing the fingers on the string;
4 drawing the string back by a few centimetres so that the fingers maintain their place on the string;
5 there is a brief pause at this point before the archer proceeds to
6 adopt an erect posture so that he can address the target;
7 a momentary pause before
8 turning the head towards the target and
9 focussing the gaze on the target to establish the line of sight, at the same time
10 concentrating the attention on the point on the target at which the shot is to be aimed.

Each of these points needs some expansion because they are fundamental to the archer making a good shot.

The hold on the bow
The size and shape of the handle of the bow dictate whether the hand can be

placed on it in one position only or in a variety of positions. In the latter case the hand must be placed on the handle in such a way that, when the bow is fully drawn, the centre of pressure of the hand on the handle is such that the bow will not turn in the hand before or after the string is released.

The hold on the bow serves only to support and direct the bow. A vicelike grip can not only put the centre of pressure in the wrong place but also generate unwanted muscular tensions in the bow arm and shoulder.

A good hold of the bow supports it from the time the archer takes it in his hand right through to the time he sets it down after shooting his arrows. It will be unchanged whether the archer is nocking the arrow, lifting the bow up to its working position, pressing it towards the target through the draw into the follow through or lowering it in readiness for nocking the next arrow.

If the archer holds his hand outstretched, palm facing him, with the fingers stretched out together and the thumb extended to the side as far as it will go, he will notice that a line down the inside of his thumb will meet a line down the centre of the first finger at a point just inside the muscle at the base of the thumb. If this point is placed centrally on the handle of the bow in line with the vertical axis the archer will see this as the point at the base of the letter V made by thumb and first finger, his wrist making the tail to convert the V into a Y. In this way pressure from the shoulder is transmitted along the arm, pressing the bow towards the target throughout the draw into the follow through.

Now this is fine for supporting the drawn bow but what happens when the string is released? The bow must be held, otherwise it will fall to the ground. The answer is to fold the first finger round the handle to secure the bow in the hand so that it does not fall, while the little finger is pointed in the general direction of the target. A significant advantage of this is that the bow is held without the vicelike pressure that generates so much physical tension. This approach can be used for both straight and shaped handles and if correctly used can counteract some disadvantages of a straight handle.

The extended fingers should be parallel with the ground. If they are seen to point upwards then the centre of pressure on the handle will be too low, while downward pointing fingers are indicative of a high centre of pressure, neither being of any advantage to the novice archer except in the unlikely case that he is using a bow designed for high or low hand positions.

Another thing to guard against when using a straight-handled bow is overlapping of the hand above the top of the handle. This is possible with a large hand on a smallish handle, and if this happens it will certainly deflect the arrow – apart from which the fletchings may tear the skin. An arrow rest fitted above the handle overcomes this, but arrow rests on pooled equipment can suffer damage that is not always accidental.

Once a good hold has been set up in this way, irrespective of the shape and

Holding the bow. The first finger retains the drawn bow while the little finger points to the target (the third finger follows the little finger while the second exerts no pressure on the handle)

size of the handle, there is no need to move the hand until the bow is put down after shooting.

Placing the arrow on the string
It is essential that once the archer has a good hold on the bow he must not move his hand until he has shot his arrows. There is no need to move hand, finger or thumb of the bow hand when placing the arrow on the string. Such movement is very common among beginners, young or old, and is very difficult to restrain until they can be convinced of the logic of it all.

In picking up the arrow to place it on the string, the greatest control is obtained by holding it between thumb and forefinger at a point just forward of the fletchings.

Until the beginner has mastered the bow the easiest way to nock the arrow is first to bring the bow in front of the body with the hand uppermost so that it becomes a sort of workbench. The arrow can then be laid on the bow and guided towards the string so that the nock ends up in the right place.

Arrows in general use today have three vanes or fletchings. It is common for the fletching that is at right angles to the slot in the nock to be of a different colour from the others. This is traditionally called the cock feather. This cock feather must be uppermost when the arrow is placed on the bow so that the arrow leaves the bow cleanly when the string is released. This stage

Placing the arrow on the string. Neither thumb nor fingers of the bow hand are used. The arrow rests on the bow while the wrist of the hand holding the arrow is in contact with the string for greater control

is best done slowly and deliberately so that it is always under control. In archery there are no contests for 'rapid fire'.

If the equipment is in good order the arrow, once nocked, will stay where it is unless the archer interferes with it. The nock should be a good fit on the bowstring, neither so slack that it just falls off nor so tight that it has to be forced off. A simple test of this is to hold the bow so that the arrow is freely suspended from the string. A brisk light tap on the string should dislodge the arrow.

Placing the fingers on the string

This is the part of the sequence that makes or mars the shot more than any other, although in the quest for perfection every stage needs to be completed with precision.

In training for target archery, from which good training for all other disciplines will spring, the fingers are placed on the string so that the first is above the arrow and the second and third below. The thumb and little finger have no part to play and can be lightly folded so that they do not get in the way. If they are forced into the palm of the hand so much tension will be generated that a clean discharge of the arrow will be impossible.

Accurate shooting depends upon the distance between the aiming eye and the nock of the arrow remaining constant for every arrow shot. The first finger must therefore be placed on the string so that it just touches the arrow. When the bow is fully drawn, this finger will be in contact with the underside of the chin so as to give this constant distance. There should be a space of 2–3mm (about ¹⁄₁₀in) between the second finger and the arrow at this initial positioning. The gap will close when the bow is drawn but is set up initially to reduce any tendency for the second finger to lift the arrow during, or on completion of, the draw.

Finger position on the string with about 3mm gap between second finger and arrow. Without the shooting tab it is easier to see what the fingers are doing

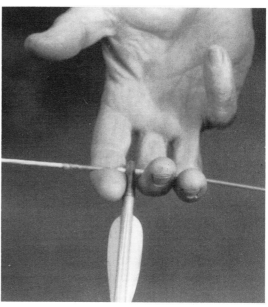

Fingers come in different lengths so anything done here must represent the best possible compromise. If an imaginary line along the axis of the arrow is extended back towards the archer his forearm, wrist and hand should lie on this line and his fingers should be parallel to it.

The next question for the archer is where the bowstring should meet each finger. Too near the fingertips and undue strain is placed on the fingers – too

Maintaining finger position on the string. The bow is drawn by about 5cm. Note the straight line from elbow through the axis of the arrow

deep a hold and a clean release is no longer possible. If the string meets the first and second fingers exactly at the crease between the first and second joints and the third finger about 5mm (⅕in) down from the first crease towards the second it will be seen that the second finger is more curved than the others as the fingers are bent to hold the string.

So far this is a 'no load' situation. To go straight from here to full draw would be to disturb the careful location of the fingers on the string which has just taken place.

Keeping the fingers in their place on the string
To make sure that the fingers stay put, the bow is drawn through about 4–5cm (1½–2in). This puts a small load on the fingers and enables the archer to go through the subsequent stages knowing that his fingers are correctly located.

But getting the fingers to stay put is not enough. They are still curved as are hand and wrist, so all are in a state of tension. Now is the time for the archer to let tension become extension by letting the fingers, hand and wrist

Preparation. The arrow is nocked but attention is still on the hands, and the shoulders are bowed

stretch and straighten while at the same time maintaining the load and the small amount of draw. In this way much of the task of maintaining this load is transferred from the arm muscles to the shoulder while the forearm, wrist, hand and fingers are on their way to becoming no more than a link from elbow to fingertips.

The pause
The pause that follows this stage is momentary – possibly only a fraction of a second – but it should exist and be seen to exist. It marks the end of the manipulative stage and precedes the establishment of a good body position, the essential preliminary to drawing the bow.

Standing erect
So far the work done has been to use the hands to hold and load the bow. The archer has concentrated his attention on what he has been doing with his hands, which are down at about waist level. As a result his head and shoulders are bent so that he can better see what he is doing. Now he has to

Standing. The new archer now stands erect looking along the shooting line. Tab and bracer have not yet been fitted; the coach thus has a better view of how the pupil uses her hands and arms

stand erect, lifting the head and straightening the spine. It helps if the gaze is fixed on the horizon or on some nearer point at eye level. It is time for the archer to draw a breath, force the air down into the diaphragm and then exhale slowly and completely.

Addressing the target

A brief pause at this point separates the actions and prevents the archer from starting the next stage before he has completed the previous one.

The archer turns his head so that his aiming eye can see the target clearly past the bridge of his nose. For precision in shooting the aiming eye must be in the same vertical plane as the nock of the arrow when the bow is fully drawn.

Establishing the line of sight

The gaze is concentrated on the target and from here onwards, until the shot is complete, this visual concentration must not be disturbed; the archer has established his line of sight from the aiming eye to the point on the target that he wishes to hit with his arrow.

In other words, if the archer is distracted at this stage and shifts his eye from the target he will need to re-establish his concentration before he goes any further.

Concentration on the target

This is not that grim determination to attain the objective regardless of cost, which some people equate with concentration; such an approach is guaranteed to produce tensions in the mind if not in the body as well. What archery requires is the kind of concentration that excludes everything not relevant to the task in hand.

The target is seen in sharp focus – after all it is the target that the archer wishes to hit with his arrow, is it not? If the target is in sharp focus – at 'infinity' in photographic terms – the bow and any attachment on it will be less than one metre (about a yard) away and therefore very much out of focus. This will include the bow sight, of which more later, but the archer will not see the bow sight at all until it comes into his field of view, which will be very narrow because of his concentration on the target.

Drawing

Drawing – drawing or bending the bow – is the one word that embraces probably the most complex sequence in the whole act of shooting an arrow from a bow.

The bow must be bent so that the energy to discharge the arrow can be stored in the limbs of the bow until the archer releases the string. If the archer wants his arrows to form a recognisable group in the target, the bow

Addressing the target. The head is turned but nothing else has moved. The line of sight is established and the pupil concentrates on the target

must store the same amount of energy for each shot. This is unvarying, regardless of the distance between archer and target.

This stored energy is the propellant for the shot – the parallel with the gun in Chapter 2. Variations in the amount by which the bow is drawn are the equivalents of variations in the propellant charge and lead to the scattering of successive shots all over the target area instead of the close groups the archer would like to achieve. There are three stages in the drawing of the bow: the presentation of the bow to the target so that the bow sight is placed on the line of sight; the bending of the bow as the string is brought into contact with the face; and the accurate location of the string and drawing hand so that the effective draw length and the relation of the nock of the arrow to the aiming eye are constant for every arrow that the archer looses – at every distance and on every day.

Presenting the bow to the target

It sounds simple enough – just lift the bow arm until the bow sight comes into the field of view and then hold it there not only until the arrow has been loosed but also beyond that until the arrow has hit the target. There is more to it than that, though, for the arm does not merely support the bow – it supplies power, direction and control in co-ordination with the other arm, the shoulders and back – and it also absorbs the shock of the discharge of the bow.

For a newcomer to the sport the most important thing will be to keep his shoulder and arm out of the path of the bowstring. He will only discover this the hard way unless the coach takes measures to prevent this during initial instruction. A good posture, once preparation is complete, will take care of the shoulder but the arm position may be more difficult to establish.

The newcomer invariably starts off with the arm locked rigid. Not only does this place the area around the elbow in the way of the bowstring, but it also creates tensions – the shoulder locks and the hand grasps the handle of the bow like a vice. In addition, when the arrow is loosed, the shock of the discharge can be absorbed only by movement of the whole arm and even of the body because of the rigidity of the arm.

There are two proven ways of correctly positioning the bow arm. The first

Presenting the bow to the target. Initial loading on the fingers is maintained but the bow is not yet drawn

is to extend the arm with the palm facing the ground. It will be seen right away that no matter how hard the hand is pressed towards the 'target' the elbow is curved out of the way of any bowstring. The wrist is then turned to bring the palm into the vertical plane. This action is reinforced by repetition with the bow in the hand.

The other way is to extend the arm with the back of the hand towards the ground and then to rotate the whole arm to bring the hand into the vertical plane, again reinforcing the idea by holding the bow when repeating the action.

With the elbow flexed in this way the bow can be pressed towards the target without straightening the arm to the extent that it obstructs the path of the bowstring. It thus contributes towards the storage of energy as the bow is drawn while giving it the direction and control called for as the string is released.

Some people will find all this very much easier than others for individual physical attributes vary considerably. Women tend to experience greater difficulty than men in positioning the bow arm so that there is a clear path for the string on the release. What must be avoided is an exaggeratedly bent elbow, for this is not only structurally unsound but also highly inefficient from the point of view of good and accurate shooting.

An exercise

A valuable exercise to familiarise the new archer with the action is for him to stand near to a door or window frame or a projecting angle of a wall so that the 'V' of the bow hand sits neatly on the angle when the arm is extended. It is essential that the hand be at or very slightly above shoulder level so that the shoulder is not forced out of position.

With the feet apart as for shooting and the shoulders in line with the arm the beginner can rotate the arm so that he can see for himself how the elbow can be moved into and out of the path of the string. Once this has been done he can press from the shoulder so that the sensation of pressing the drawn bow towards the target is developed. It is important that this results from the action of the muscles – the arm must not support any body weight. Since the wall or door frame will not move, there will be an extra sensation in this exercise, that of the body being pressed away from the support.

Bending the bow

This is Ascham's 'drawing'. So far there has been only enough loading on the string to keep the fingers in position on it during the transition from preparation to presentation.

Now the load has to be increased so that the string moves towards the face. At this stage it is tempting to tell the archer to pull the string back. *Wrong* – 'pulling' implies use of the arm muscles, particularly those of the forearm,

45

rather than those of the upper arm, shoulder and back, and thus works against the concept of the linkage between elbow and fingertips. Tell a new archer to 'pull' and see at once how the tension builds up in hand, wrist and forearm.

What matters is the elbow and how it is made to move. The operative word is 'push'. The back elbow is pushed away from the target, the initial movement continuing until the string is in contact with the face. For many people this will represent the limit for rearward movement of the string and it is here that anatomical individuality will assert itself. The infinite variation in the combinations of facial dimensions, lengths of forearm, upper arm and breadth of shoulders and even length of neck all have a bearing on the final position of bowstring and back elbow before the string leaves the fingers.

The ideal is to have the back elbow in the same vertical plane as the arrow but — largely for anatomical reasons — this is rarely achieved, even by experienced archers. Today more archers are approaching this ideal more closely as coaching knowledge and expertise have developed over the years and as more archers have committed themselves to putting a greater measure of constructive effort into their shooting.

For the new archer the question is of how to work towards this ideal. The first contact between the string and the face is not the signal for the rearward push of the elbow to stop. Even if further rearward movement of the string is imperceptible because it is now in contact with the face the work done by the muscles linked to the upper arm, shoulder and back must not diminish. At the very least it must maintain the status quo; anything less will signify a surrender to the power of the bow and then not only will contact between string and face be lost but the forces pressing the bow towards the target will also weaken, causing at best a 'dead' loose and more probably something not far removed from a total collapse.

Once the string has made contact with the face, the back and shoulder muscles come into action more and more so that the point of the elbow is brought as nearly as possible into line with the arrow as viewed from above or from behind.

More exercises

New archers have difficulty in getting their shoulders to work properly, or fail to appreciate how their back and shoulder muscles should feel when they have effective control over the bow.

One exercise that concentrates on the front shoulder, ensuring that it does not become thrust forward and/or upward is executed in the following manner:

a)   stand, hands to sides, with both feet on the shooting line so as to face the target, and focus the gaze on the target

b) keeping the elbow tucked into the side, raise the bow arm until it is parallel with the ground and the fingers are pointing towards the target

c) keep the gaze on the target and the fingers pointed towards it and at the same time slowly shuffle the feet round until they are in the normal shooting position

d) close the eyes and *feel* what is happening at the shoulder. The shoulder is automatically held back and down as it should be for effective shooting

e) the archer will find that he will be able to raise the bow arm, extending and pressing it towards the target without any movement of the shoulder.

Another complementary exercise works upon both shoulders. Here the archer will stand astride the shooting line with his hands to the sides looking straight along the shooting line to the horizon. He can then commence the exercise by:

a) raising both arms above the head, pointing straight up

b) while keeping the forearms vertical, lower the arms until the elbows are level with the ears

c) let the hands go limp so that they flop forward

d) keep the elbows at the same level while pushing them back as far as they will go

e) shut the eyes so that what happens at the back and shoulders can be felt.

This exercise can be continued so as to reproduce some of the sensations of actually drawing the bow and of the follow through:

f) turn the head to address the target

g) bring the arms down to the shooting position

h) take the arms into the follow through position.

This again can be reinforced if the archer closes his eyes.

Exercises like this may seem mildly eccentric but, because they reproduce in static form something of what happens during the act of drawing the bow and releasing the arrow, they are of considerable value. They are of even more value in dealing with problems arising from incorrect posture because the archer has to stand erect before he can attempt these exercises.

Holding

This takes the making of the shot into the holding stage, that interval between the string making contact with the face and arrival at the point of no return when the string must leave the fingers. It is during this interval that the archer has his last chance to make a quick mental assessment that everything feels right as he steadies the aim and builds up the effort into the loose and follow through. If things do not feel as they should, the archer can still let down, lower his hands, return the arrow to the quiver and start all over again.

It is difficult to say how long this holding period might be – it depends on the wind, the environment, the archer's assessment of the feel of things, the state of his concentration. It will vary fractionally from arrow to arrow and it would be unwise to say how long the interval ought to be. It is better to say that it should not be prolonged unnecessarily. Anything in excess of seven seconds, if repeated at every shot, will generate undue fatigue accompanied by a breakdown of concentration. Observation of thousands of archers suggests that today something like four seconds is typical. This is not a drill movement, to be repeated mechanically for every arrow regardless of environmental and other factors. The string will leave when the archer is ready for it to leave, consciously or unconsciously, if all that has led up to this stage has been done well.

While the archer retains his concentration on the target he is gently and steadily increasing both the forces pressing the bow towards the target and the forces that take the back elbow round as nearly in line with the arrow as is

The draw complete. The pupil maintains pressure on the bow towards the target, while pushing the back elbow to the rear

physically possible. At the same time the link between elbow and fingertips is stretching and straightening as the initial tension in this link becomes extension.

Finally the fingers are so stretched that they can no longer retain the string and the release occurs.

Loosing

This is the traditional term for the release of the string. Folklore has it that it can be controlled, but by the time it happens no control is possible. The control is exercised by the care taken in the preparation and in the proper use of the body in presenting the bow to the target and in bending the bow.

The knowledgeable onlooker can see the state of affairs before the loose, noting the final relationship of the fingers to string and arrow. He would also note any tensions existing in the archer's fingers, hand, wrist and forearm – or indeed elsewhere. After the release there are in the follow through many tell-tale signs of how well the archer has prepared the shot and of whether he has stopped working on it before the loose or has continued applying effort into the follow through.

The follow through

This is something Ascham never committed to print, but today it plays a vital part in good shooting. It is said by many coaches that the follow through is the most important part of the loose. It is now recognised that the loose is a momentary event where the string leaves the fingers some time between developing the hold and arriving at the follow through.

In archery the follow through is defined as the maintenance of the concentration and line of sight as they existed before the string was released while holding the body, arms and hands in the position in which they came to rest after the loose. The good archer holds this follow through until the arrow has hit the target and then for that vital additional fraction of a second during which he assesses the shot and any variations in the way he made it. The hands are then lowered and the archer pauses before doing anything more.

If the archer has further arrows to shoot he will take up the next arrow and repeat the sequence.

Filling the gaps

Up to now only a passing mention has been made of string location at the face, while aiming has been totally ignored. This is deliberate; the former is so dependent upon individual characteristics that it needs to be considered separately rather than as a stage in the sequence, while the latter could almost be developed into a chapter in its own right.

Apart from this it is better that the archer develops control over his bow at

The follow through. Concentration on the target is maintained, while the arms are still held where they ended up after the shot

close range, shooting at a bare target boss, before the complications of aiming and scoring are introduced. Too early a concentration on sights, scoring (or the proximity of the shot to the gold) and the visual aspects of shooting take the mind off posture and preparation.

String location at the face

For countless years this has been termed the 'anchor point' with the corresponding verb 'to anchor'; the implications of this are that everything stops when the string reaches it and that it is a solid, immovable thing, to be felt as a substantial force applied to the face.

This is somewhat at variance with the real needs of the archer. Assuming that the head is correctly positioned, the archer will need to bring the string to make contact with his chin at a point so that the nock of the arrow is in the same vertical plane as the aiming eye. With a constant head position for every shot, the string must also be brought to the same reference point on the face every time the bow is drawn, so that the archer gives himself the greatest possible chance of repeating exactly what he has done before.

50

*Before and after the loose. Andrew
Scott of Scarborough, Yorkshire, at
the 1987 UK Masters Tournament*

Vertical alignment is not all; for consistent shooting the distance between the nock of the arrow and the aiming eye must also be a constant. The archer achieves this through contact between the forefinger of the drawing hand and the underside of the jaw, contact being made at the same point for every shot.

The starting point for all this is to have the archer bring the string to the centre of his chin and to position the head so that the string just touches the tip of his nose as a secondary reference point. This is the easiest set of reference points to find consistently, which is why it is chosen as a starting point. However it is by no means the end of the story.

The archer may not feel comfortable even though he cannot say exactly why. Only the coach can see this and assess the reasons for the apparent discomfort. It may be that it is just the newness of the activity and that the discomfort will go as the archer settles in to the act of shooting. On the other hand the physical characteristics of the archer (the shape and size of his face, the breadth of his shoulders or the length of his arms) might account for his discomfort. Assessment by the coach might lead to the reference point being moved from centre to side of the chin, but there is no rule to guide anyone because of the infinitive variety of individual dimensions.

If such a change is made, both archer and coach must work together to ensure that the necessary conditions for accurate shooting are still met. This would be less difficult for the experienced archer than for the novice who has still to learn how things feel when he is making good shots. One thing must be remembered; with a reference point at the side of the chin the contact of the forefinger under the jaw may be difficult to establish with any certainty. Hence some artificial means of creating an equivalent contact must be introduced so that the distance from nock to eye cannot vary. Similarly there has to be a change in head position so that eye and nock are kept in the same vertical plane.

String picture

This is a rather fanciful term for the visual alignment of the string with the bow. It is all part of the establishment of constant head position with constant reference points to set up the vertical distance between eye and nock and keeping the nock vertically below the eye.

If the target is seen in sharp focus (as it should be) and the bow sight out of focus, but with reasonable clarity, the string, being so much closer to the face, will only be seen as a very blurred image that lines up with the edge of the cut out of the handle section of the bow.

This alignment is important in reducing the lateral scatter of the hits on the target, which would otherwise occur.

Aiming

The line of sight has already been mentioned – it is that straight line between

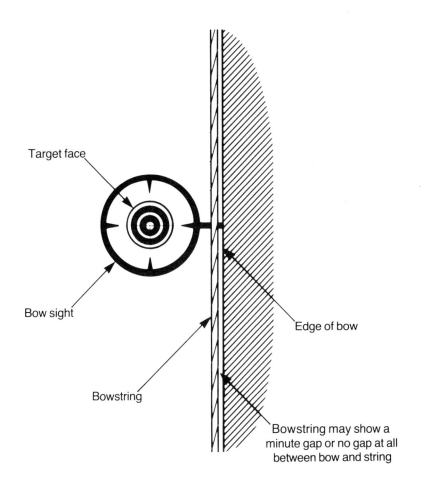

Target face

Bow sight

Bowstring

Edge of bow

Bowstring may show a
minute gap or no gap at all
between bow and string

String picture

the aiming eye and the point on the target at which the archer aims. So, if the point at which the archer aims is not the exact centre of a target consisting of concentric scoring zones, he can hardly blame equipment or environment if his group of shots is also not central on the target.

The bow sight is set so that the archer gives the right amount of elevation for his shots to strike centrally on the target, neither too high nor too low. Once the archer has developed a consistent shooting form he can calibrate his bow sight so that he knows whereabouts on the vertical track he has to set the sight attachment to give the necessary elevation for any distance at which he is called upon to shoot.

In practice it is not quite as simple as this. Every field used for archery has its own environment, different from any other. So shooting on one field will differ from shooting elsewhere in one way or another, and the sight calibration for shooting on one field will always differ very slightly from that required for shooting on another. Furthermore the weather differs from one day to the next and this in turn will have its effect on the calibration.

This is one reason why it is built into the rules of target archery that before any sort of competition, from club target day up to major contests, a prescribed number of sighter arrows is permitted before the archers begin to shoot for scores.

The coach will insist on the archer thinking in terms of shooting recognisable groups in the target, rather than in terms of the scoring values of the individual arrows. With training this can be developed into shooting tighter and tighter groups of arrows.

When the archer can repeatedly produce unmistakable groups of arrows he will be firmly established on the road to success. Furthermore, if these groups are not quite central on the target then adjustment of the bow sight should bring them into the centre.

The golden rules for sight adjustment are:

1   Never make adjustments on the basis of one or two arrows
2   Group high on the target – move sight *up* to bring the group down towards the centre
3   Group low on the target – move sight *down* to bring the group up towards the centre
4   Group left on the target – move sight *left* to move the group towards the centre
5   Group right on the target – move sight *right* to move the group towards the centre
6   Be positive in adjustment – for vertical adjustments move the sight by about 5mm (⅕in) for the first adjustment and then continue or return by smaller amounts if necessary. Moving the sight by a fraction of a millimetre at a time will not have any significant effect on group location and will be just a waste of time.
7   For large lateral adjustments, a slight shift of foot position will achieve more than will fiddling with the bow sight. For a group to the left of the centre pointing the whole body more to the right and vice versa should do the job. Then, and only then make use of the bow sight movement for the fine adjustment, again erring on the generous side before continuing in the same direction or reversing the movement.
8   Major left-right errors in particular may be due to defective shooting technique, but if the errors are constant leave them alone while in competition. Leave technique untouched until you can arrange to discuss it with your coach in training sessions.

CHAPTER FIVE

Putting it into practice

Very few archers start off completely on their own – apart from children cutting bows from the hedgerows or borrowing their parents' garden canes. Beyond this stage, entry into the sport may be via club or sports centre, through tasting it at an activity holiday or through a demonstration combined with a 'have a go' session at a country fair.

The shooting technique described in the previous chapter has to be put together in reality and this is where the coach or instructor enters the picture. The would-be archer has only two hands, one for holding the bow and the other for controlling the string so that he cannot at the same time hold the book open at the right page. Likewise if he is concentrating his attention on the target he cannot simultaneously read the printed word. The coach has to guide the archer in handling the equipment, in positioning the body and the limbs at each stage and in getting the sequence in the right order.

Learning to shoot in the bow is very much like learning to drive a car. The pupil sits behind the wheel with his feet at the pedals driving while learning how to drive and at the same time assimilating essential roadcraft. There is no other way in which it can be done.

So it is with the archer: he stands on the shooting line in front of the target, drawing the bow and loosing the arrows while learning how to do these things and absorbing some of the atmosphere of the sport. There can be no instant achievement. Instead the archer progressively builds up each stage while putting the steps together to create a smoothly working sequence, a process that might be measured in days, weeks or even months.

A person starting off in a club, in an almost one-to-one relationship with his coach at sessions of at least two hours' duration twice weekly might attain a level of performance in two or three weeks surpassing that of a year's efforts at a sports centre where, under a single instructor, a group of ten meets once weekly for a 45min session. Does it matter, though, provided both kinds of archer enjoy what they are doing?

The rate of progress is very much in the hands of the would-be archer. The coach advises, encourages and guides. Any goals set must be readily attainable; it is useless talking about Master Bowmen when the archer can barely group his arrows at a range of 20m, but the coach can talk about getting similar grouping at 30 or 40m or getting much tighter groups at 20m.

The starting point

Any sort of 'taster' shows the would-be archer the enjoyment he can get; at the same time the coach sees whether the pupil has a natural flair for shooting or whether there has to be a slow and painstaking process towards achieving control of body and bow.

Now the work must start. In a sports centre the group will almost certainly be of mixed ability. New members may be side by side with those who have been attending for a year or so. Because of the layout in the sports hall and the pressure on both time and space, introductory techniques available in the club cannot be used and the newcomer will have to begin shooting with the rest of the group.

In a club the new archer often has the coach to himself and works from quite a different beginning.

New archers are welcome

It takes a while for a coach to get to know his pupil even in a one-to-one relationship – and very much longer if the pupil is one of a group at a sports centre.

The coach may be an awe-inspiring figure but, nevertheless, he is an archer committed to bringing in the next generation of archers to the sport. His approach determines whether his pupils become interested and want to go further or will just complete the requisite number of sessions and then disappear. Indoors or outside, the coach has to create a welcoming atmosphere so that all start off with a spirit of co-operation.

The golden rule is for the coach to be at the appointed place well before the commencement of the session so that all necessary equipment is set out before the pupils arrive. Likewise for the pupils, it is good form to arrive on time – nothing is worse in a short session than having to go back to the beginning for the benefit of latecomers.

Names are important. A general introduction makes a good start in the welcoming process, followed by a brief outline of the objectives. Is everybody wearing suitable clothing? Who is right- or left-handed? Then the pointing exercise – the coach needs to know if eye dominance is likely to be a problem for anyone. The coach does not have to mention the words, but he has to know so that he can anticipate problems. An archer who shoots with the bow in his left hand is known as a right-handed archer and vice versa. This convention is used throughout the sport.

Introducing the equipment

Now the coach can introduce the equipment the archers are going to use – not the flamboyant weapons used by film or television characters nor the complex items illustrated in the catalogues for these are not relevant. The watchword is 'keep it simple'. New archers need to know the names of the things they are going to use, and – at this stage – nothing more.

This equipment is not in a showcase – it is there to be used – but it comes in different sizes. Each member of the group in turn must be assessed for the size and weight of bow most appropriate to his physique, bearing in mind that the range of pooled equipment is rarely extensive. It helps if the bows can be numbered; 'bow no 7' is more easily remembered than 'the red bow drawing 25lb at 28in'. It is the same with arrows – most likely they will be just as purchased by the club or sports centre. At this stage they are not easy to identify for size, so it is worth the effort of colour coding their cresting according to arrow length, with varied fletching colours to distinguish different sets of the same length. Extra work for the coach, but it makes life easier and can help prevent a new archer from accidentally using arrows that are too short for him.

Initially in assessing a person for arrow length it will suffice for the nock of a long arrow or measuring stick to be placed against the upper part of the archer's chest (near the top of the breastbone) in line with the shoulders and

Using a marked arrow for initial assessment of arrow length for a new archer

A more accurate assessment of arrow length once the new archer has some control over the bow

for the archer to stretch both arms out in front of him so that the arrow is held between the outstretched fingers. About 2in (5cm) beyond the fingertips will be the first approximation for arrow length, allowing a reasonable margin of safety against overdrawing (drawing the arrow inside the bow through lack of proper control). Once consistent shooting form has been established the archer can draw a measuring arrow in his bow so that a more accurate assessment can be made of the suitable arrow length.

This is the time to issue bracers. Again it is sensible to have them numbered – it saves arguments, especially if there are several young people in the group. Finger tabs can wait – a tab cannot very well be trimmed to suit any individual since it will be used by someone else in the next session, and in any case both coach and archer have a need to see what the fingers are doing. Once the archer has made sufficient progress to justify the use of a tab he would be well advised to buy one.

Most clubs can supply bow stands and ground quivers, but these are rare in sports centres. Bows and arrows in sports centres must therefore be placed on the floor of the archery range when not in use, and the coach must emphasise the need for careful and disciplined handling.

The first arrows

The first arrows the archer will shoot will probably not be at the target but into the ground just over three yards (about three metres) from his feet or – in a sports hall – at a target boss leaning against the wall.

The idea is to overcome that very real fear of loosing the arrow, so often seen when the archer is obliged to loose his first arrows from a fully drawn bow directly at the target. Loosing into the ground is a valuable coaching aid. The bow does not have to be drawn fully but it is drawn in full view of both archer and coach and the archer can see and feel for himself just how fingers, hands and arms are used. In this exercise the hold on the bow does not have to be precise as it would for actual shooting, while neither posture nor the placing of the feet are of great importance so long as the archer can do what is required of him.

The archer learns to lay the arrow on the bow, holding it just forward of the fletchings and guiding the nock onto the bowstring. The coach can then show how the fingers are placed on the string and the load applied to keep them in place. Demonstration is easy when the coach is equipped with a similar bow and arrows.

The coach guides the pupil into pressing the bow away from him towards the intended point of impact while at the same time pushing back with the other elbow so that the hands separate more and more as the bow is drawn. Once the bow is drawn through about half to two-thirds of the arrow length, the pupil can let his fingers stretch and straighten quite slowly until the string leaves the fingers. The exercise is repeated a number of times to reinforce the lesson while the pupil is encouraged to maintain the pressure on the bow and the backward push of the elbow right through the action of letting the fingers straighten into a follow through.

Pupils should watch attentively both before and after their turn so that they have a greater appreciation of what happens. For this stage it is important to have the fingers, hand, wrist and forearm in line with the axis of the arrow, whether seen from the side or from above.

The body

The next job is to give the group a sense of body position. It helps if a shooting line is laid down on the field (in a sports hall there is usually a choice of lines). The pupils can then stand astride the line with their bow hands towards the target area, allowing enough space between each archer for the equipment to lie at their feet.

They will face along the line so that the coach can correct the posture. He will be looking at the placing of the feet and for signs of tension, uneven weight distribution, hunching of the shoulders and anything else that might affect efficient use of the body when shooting.

Posture assured, the whole group can then mime the placing of the arms under the direction of the coach. The group simulates the actions of addressing the target, presenting the bow to the target and of drawing the bow under 'no load' conditions, and thus develops a sense of position before having to cope with the bow at the same time. Once the group has mastered the mimed action, a few repetitions with the eyes closed are a useful reinforcement.

There is a nice ball and socket joint at each shoulder so that, both in mime and in reality, there is no reason why the arms cannot be raised freely without any lift of the shoulders. It requires practice – this action is only called for in archery and the body has to get used to it. It is important that the arms are raised to just a little above shoulder height – the act of drawing the bow can then be used to keep the shoulders back and down.

Archers have to shoot

No first session can end without each member of the group having shot at least three arrows at the target. This makes considerable demands on both coach and archers if the session is limited to one hour or less. Under these conditions the instructor cannot insist that everything is done correctly before moving on to the next stage. If the idea is there and the new archer is seen to be safe that must do for the first session. Refinement must wait until subsequent sessions.

The mimed action must be followed by action with the bow in the hand but as yet without the arrow. Sequence is important and no one can be allowed to get away with short cuts. This is the first time that the group members experience the weight of the drawn bow. The benefits of the preparatory exercises should now be evident.

This is when the hold on the bow will first be seen to matter. If the wrist is turned in, the front arm will be in the path of the bowstring and the arm will tend to lock. If the wrist is turned out, the weight of the bow will be taken on the thumb and the action will be structurally weak, apart from any physical damage that might result. The instructor's priority is to deal with these things before worrying too much about high or low wrists, important as they are for good shooting.

A few essays at drawing the bow without an arrow should consolidate the action sufficiently for the group to proceed with shooting. The archer will know what to expect from the bow and will have found the reference point on his face where the string makes contact.

Loading the bow – or as archers would say, nocking an arrow – is a surprisingly difficult hurdle for the novice to clear. In spite of the coach emphasising repeatedly the need for a constant correct hold on the bow and in spite of as much preliminary drill as time will allow, the novice will insist on moving his hand on the handle of the bow when he first nocks his arrows. It is common for the novice to hold the bow so that the thumb sticks up at its side and then to lay the arrow between the bow and his thumb. Once the arrow has been nocked the novice will again move his hand – this time to a hold that is approximately correct but with one big difference – the index finger is used to hold the arrow against the bow. Only as he begins to put a load on the string does he realise that he has pulled the string out of the nock and that he is still holding the arrow with his finger.

It is a constant struggle for the coach to iron out these 'instinctive' bad habits, but eradicated they must be and as soon as possible. From the work study point of view they are unnecessary, inefficient and often unsafe, and yet they recur with each intake of new archers until the coach has convinced them that the arrow will rest on the bow without help from thumb or forefinger of the bow hand.

The exercise of loosing into the ground should have established the positioning of the fingers on the bowstring – but do not take this for granted. The fear of loosing has probably been overcome but never be too sure – even if it has, the new archer will still tend to clench his fingers round the string. If he does (and the movement can sometimes be almost imperceptible) he will almost certainly twist the bowstring and take the arrow off the rest as he does so. Arrow rests with a curved tip are a snare and a delusion – with such a crutch the archer may never fully learn to control his fingers on the bowstring.

When the arrow is twisted off the string in this way there is only one thing to do: *stop*, let the bow down gently, remove the arrow from the string and begin again. The instruction from the coach: 'come down!' is one that should be understood from the outset. For the sake of safety it is a very important command.

Another characteristic of the novice is that of combining the action of addressing the target with that of drawing the bow while forgetting to put the body in the right position in the first place. If done at speed this will throw the arrow off the rest, but even if not, it will result in a hunched and unstable body position where back and shoulder muscles have no chance of being used effectively.

In a class where everyone starts from scratch the coach can give frequent reminders about sequence, posture and position. With a mixed ability group he not only has to worry about beginners, but also has to keep his eye open for signs of backsliding by those who should know better.

All archers want some sort of target to shoot at, irrespective of the particular aspect of the sport they wish to follow. For initial instruction a specific target is an encumbrance – it diverts the beginner's attention from the immediate goal of achieving control of body and bow to the ultimately desirable goal of hitting the centre of the target.

A completely bare target boss set up at about 5m from the shooting line is ideal for the shooting of the very first arrows. It cuts out a lot of walking and it means also that the new archers can safely be guided to shoot with their eyes shut, thus learning to recognise what it *feels* like when drawing the bow. If the archers can go through this process they will be better prepared for what comes next, with a degree of body awareness that leads to better control of the bow.

This exercise can be extended to develop the sense of elevation or depression by pivoting the body at the hips so that the relation of the head, shoulders, arms and the upper part of the body remains constant at any degree of elevation or depression. This action is spoken of as 'unit aiming', for the head, shoulders, arms and upper body are moved together *as a single unit* to direct the aim according to the distance at which the archer is shooting.

In outdoor target archery, clout shooting and for longer or uphill shots in field archery control of elevation is important, while in indoor target archery

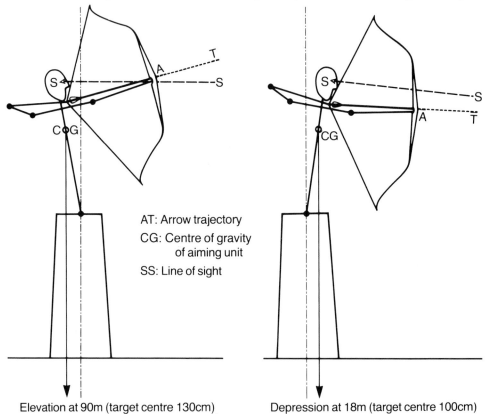

AT: Arrow trajectory
CG: Centre of gravity
     of aiming unit
SS: Line of sight

Elevation at 90m (target centre 130cm)   Depression at 18m (target centre 100cm)

Unit aiming

and for downhill and very short range shots in field archery the less commonly experienced need for controlling depression comes to the fore.

It soon becomes evident that individual rates of progress are very variable. This is the excitement and challenge that attracts archers into the art of coaching. It is a constant endeavour to make the learning process easy and enjoyable for the new archer while at the same time leading him to achieve skilful control of the bow.

Withdrawing arrows

Arrows shot into a target have to be pulled out before they can be shot again – they are not expendable. As with everything in archery this must be done safely and effectively.

The tendency, especially among young people, to crowd round the target and grab the arrows without steadying the target boss must be checked from the outset. There is danger if the job is not done properly.

Take an example where one archer only has shot three arrows into the target. The archer *walks* up to the target (archers never, never run where there is archery equipment of any kind about) and then approaches from the side so that his bow arm is farthest from the target. He places the back of his drawing hand flat against the target face with the nearest arrow between his fingers. The bow hand is then placed over the arrow to grasp it firmly as close to the target as possible.

By standing sideways to the target he can see that the area immediately behind the arrow is clear of bystanders and can use his body most effectively to remove the arrow without risking damage to either arrow or target face.

He places the arrow he has just withdrawn between the thumb and the palm of the hand against the target and moves to the next nearest arrow where he repeats the process before moving on to the third arrow. The archer can hold a dozen or more arrows in this way without difficulty.

Imagine that instead of one archer with three arrows only there are six archers each with six arrows in the target – the most that will be encountered in any archery event. If one archer at a time pulls only his own arrows he has to lean over someone else's arrows and thus risk damaging them in order to get at his own.

If every archer of the six is withdrawing his own arrows the first archer must stop when he can no longer easily reach his own shafts and let the next archer in, returning only when it is clear for him to do so. This is complicated.

An alternative, with the consent of all archers on the target, is for one person to pull all the arrows, passing them back for distribution to their respective owners. Today this is accepted as the better way provided that the distribution is done systematically – some archers at tournaments seem to do the job more quickly and efficiently than others. The important thing is not

to conduct a post-mortem at the target but to return promptly to the shooting line so as not to hold up the shooting.

In the open, especially at longer distances, some arrows may miss the target. If they are in front of the target they should be picked up as the archers advance so that they are not trampled upon. The method of withdrawing the arrow from the ground is similar to that of pulling it from the target.

The archer approaches the arrow from the side and bends his knees to reach it, keeping the back as upright as possible. The bow hand is used to grasp the arrow as near to the pile as possible while the other hand is used to steady the arrow and stabilise the squatting position. The arrow is gently eased from the ground. Any soil clinging to the arrow should be wiped off immediately. If the arrow is lying flat and partly buried in the grass rather than sticking up at an angle it will be necessary to part the grass so that the entire length of the arrow can be seen before lifting it clear.

Partly buried arrows are difficult to find and constantly cause delays at tournaments. Every club should invest in a metal detector and, apart from home use, take it to any tournament where club members are shooting.

Introducing aiming

Even before they have shot many beginners in archery ask how they should aim. From the television and the cinema they will have some idea of how a rifle is used – they see backsights, foresights and telescopic sights mounted on the gun and the marksman looking along the barrel. When it comes to the bow they are at a loss; no barrel, no backsight and – with the training bow – no apparent foresight. Small wonder, then, that the untutored novice will try and bring the arrow up to eye level and look along it. The coach thus has to do some explaining.

Since he is answering the beginner's question the answer has to be simple and straightforward, though it will need to be expanded and reinforced later.

For the archer the aiming eye *is* the backsight.

The foresight is mounted on the bow and can be adjusted for elevation or depression. Accurate aiming depends on the bow sight being placed on the line of sight between aiming eye and target centre, while the nock of the arrow is brought to the same point in relation to the aiming eye for every arrow the archer shoots.

(opposite, above) *Withdrawing arrows. The back of the hand against the target with arrows already pulled held by the thumb. Here the archer steadies the target with his bow hand so that his body does not obstruct the photographer by casting a shadow*

(opposite, below) *Withdrawing arrows. The archer has placed his free hand over the arrow and is ready to pull it from the target*

That having been said, it is put into the background until the beginner has been taught how to handle his equipment and has been through the stages leading to control of body and bow. Now it is time to introduce aiming in more detail.

Where an adult is using pooled training equipment and shooting at 15 to 20m a good first approximation is for the coach to use his own eye-to-chin distance as the distance above the arrow rest for setting the sight pin. The pin is inserted in the foam strip so that its head is just seen protruding beyond the side of the bow.

In use the archer takes his place on the shooting line, nocks the arrow, stands upright and addresses the target. His attention is concentrated on the target to set up the line of sight and the bow is lifted until the bow sight (the pin head) appears in his now quite narrow field of view. If this is done properly he will have no need to (and must not) look for the sight. It will come into his field of view in such a way that very little if any adjustment of body position will be required to bring the pin onto line of sight.

If it seems that much vertical adjustment of body position is called for, the archer must apply the 'unit aiming' technique, pivoting the body unit at the hips as in the parallel with the gun.

Suppose that the first shot hits the target at the bottom instead of in the centre. There will be a great temptation to alter the sight immediately. Resist it! Who can say that in all respects that arrow was shot correctly?

With a new archer anything may happen – he often masters one element of the desired shooting form while omitting another. Even with experienced and usually competent archers odd things can happen if concentration is disturbed. Wait and see what happens with the second shot. If it lands in much the same place as the first there could be reasonable grounds for adjustment, provided that both shots were made in exactly the same way.

On the other hand, both shots may have been slightly out of control so again the temptation to adjust the sight should be resisted; the archer should wait and see what happens to the third shot. If this ends up close to the first two then these shots will form a recognisable group. Sight adjustment then becomes a necessity to bring the group from the bottom of the target to the centre.

The method of adjustment is to leave the sight unaltered until the archer next takes his place on the shooting line. He then holds his bow out as when presenting it to the target for shooting and places the bow sight on his line of sight. He can see in his field of view the location of his arrows and can assess where on his bow this group appears to be relative to the sight. By moving his sight down to that position he will increase the elevation when he next shoots and will thus have moved his group from the bottom of the target to a point much closer to the centre. The amount of adjustment will usually be several millimetres rather than a fraction of a millimetre. The rule is:

Group below centre – move sight down – increase elevation
Group above centre – move sight up – decrease elevation

Consistent errors to the left or to the right are often the result of errors in the archer's shooting technique or in the set-up of his equipment rather than of inefficient sight setting, and manifest themselves when the sight has to be pushed in so far that the archer can no longer see it or when it has to be pushed out so far that something is patently wrong.

This is no help to the archer who wants immediate action to bring the group to the centre from, say, the left hand side of the target. Body alignment is the lateral equivalent of elevation and depression so the traversing mechanism has to be called into play.

For the novice archer this is where foot markers can be useful. If foot markers (golf tees are ideal for outdoor use – or pieces of coloured self-adhesive tape on the floor indoors) are placed at the archer's toes before he starts to shoot the feet can be moved to change body alignment. In the case of a group to the left of centre the archer would move his front foot a little to the right or the back foot a little to the left so that the body points more to the right than previously. The feet are fractionally turned so that comfort is maintained and the foot markers are moved to new positions at the archer's toes. The amount of movement is small – moving one foot by about an inch – 2cm – while keeping the other still may prove to be more than enough. Experienced competitive archers make this movement instinctively without aids to location because in their training and practice their sense of body alignment has become very well developed. They take up their position on the line and adjust it as necessary without even being aware that they are doing it.

Bracing the bow
With beginners it will help for the first few sessions if the coach braces all the bows before the start of the session. Not only does it give the beginners more time but it ensures also that the job is done correctly – likewise with unbracing the bows afterwards.

Sooner or later, though, the beginner will have to master this important task. Even adults with comparatively light bows find it difficult to brace a bow correctly without applying a lot of unnecessary effort in their early attempts. For them it is a struggle accompanied by much puffing and panting. This is due to misunderstanding of the directions in which the forces are applied and of where they are applied, coupled with the need to have the fingers of the hand on the upper limb free to manipulate the string into and out of the nock on the bow.

Practice should always begin with a light bow. The bottom limb of the bow with the string already in place in the nock is located against the instep so that the pressure from the bow is at right angles to the foot. The lower

Bracing a simple bow. The bow is bent sufficiently for the string to remain slack until the loop is safely positioned in the nock

bow tip must always be clear of the ground so that it does not get covered in soil (a natural abrasive that can wear away the loop of the bowstring quite quickly). If the pressure from the bow is not at right angles to the foot the bow can easily slip with sometimes painful consequences. The next stage is the placing of the other foot – the feet should be parallel and fairly wide apart so that the archer looking downwards will see the handle of the bow between the feet. The hand nearest to the lower limb holds the handle with the elbow firmly against the body. The heel of the other hand is placed on the upper limb so that the fingers are free to guide the loop. The arm is locked rigid with the shoulder moved forward so that should the hand slip the bow limb would strike the shoulder area and not the face.

The body is tilted from the hips towards the upper limb of the bow so that the hand on the handle pulls upwards while the other hand bears down on the upper limb to bend the bow. As the bow bends the hand slides up towards the nock with the fingers guiding the loop until it slips into place in the nock. A check is made with the fingers to ensure that the loop is firmly in place, after which the archer can relax and turn the bow in his hand so that the string is uppermost. Now he can check visually that the string is secure in both nocks and in line with the centre of the bow.

Unbracing the bow is the same procedure in reverse. Feet, hands and body are positioned as for bracing the bow and the body again tilted towards the upper limb so that the bow bends and the string becomes slack. The tip of the index finger is placed in the vee of the loop (on the farther side of the bow from the archer) and follows the loop round until it is completely free from the nock. The archer gently eases off the pressure and the string slides down the bow.

At one time this was the only way to brace and unbrace bows, although another method had to be employed when steel bows were commonplace in the 1950s.

Today, although the method described above can be used with recurve bows *in an emergency* it is not kind to them. The cord bowstringer is in universal use. It consists of a short leather sleeve fitted over the nock in which the bowstring is already placed. At the other end of the cord is a saddle with a non-slip rubber face. This is placed on the other limb of the bow as near the tip as possible but with the free loop between the saddle and the nock. The cord is long enough for the foot to be placed on its centre while the archer pulls the bow up by the handle. In this way the bow is bent sufficiently for the loop to be guided into the nock by the archer's free hand. The pressure is eased off and again the prudent archer will make a visual check that all is well.

Unbracing is a similar process, the stringer being used as before to bend the bow and slacken the string so that the loop can be removed from the nock.

The length of the cord can be adjusted to suit both bow and archer, but it should be long enough to allow reasonable downward components of the forces bending the bow. At the same time it should not be so long that the archer has difficulty in bending the bow enough for the string to be put into its working position.

CHAPTER SIX

The competitive archer

It will not be long before the new archer begins to think about competition. The big question will be 'how?' and the answers will be many and varied.

Openings will be most limited for the once-a-week archer at the local sports centre – the most that can usually be arranged is an end of term contest between members of the group, although once some level of consistent performance has been reached it might be possible to relate the short range scores to the handicap schemes devised by the national governing body. For young people in the United Kingdom there is the badge scheme of the Association for Archery in Schools (AAS) in which both the white and blue badges can be shot for indoors at 20yd using a 60cm target face, always provided that there is enough time for shooting 36 arrows in ends of three. (An 'end' is the number of arrows each archer shoots before the signal is given for scoring and collection of arrows – usually three arrows indoors and at short outdoor ranges and six arrows at the longer outdoor distances.)

School archery often has similar limits on time though extension is possible in preparation for an inter-school match or for entry in an AAS tournament.

The greatest opportunity for competition exists in the club. Once the newcomer to the sport has achieved a certain level of control over body and bow, he will want to take his place on the line with the more established club members and attempt the same routines that they have been following for a long time.

Here several kinds of competition are possible. The fundamental one is that of competition with himself – monitoring his scores at the end of shooting and comparing them with previous scores, and relating the scores at one distance with those at other distances using the GNAS handicap tables. In this way the British archer can assess for himself whether he is continuing to make progress, has reached a (hopefully temporary) plateau or whether some problem is showing itself in a downward trend.

Where several people have entered archery at about the same time, the group identity will be strong, with a nice spirit of friendly rivalry and of mutual help should performance take a downward turn. In due time, too, there will be the thought of approaching, ultimately equalling and perhaps even surpassing the performance of the longer established membership.

The basis of competition

For competition to be effective the conditions in which shooting takes place must be equal for all, allowing no competitor to gain advantage over the others save by his own skill with the bow. This is where the rules of shooting come in. They provide for safety at all times when shooting is in progress, define nature and control of the competition and of equipment used and set out to prevent one competitor gaining an unfair advantage over another and to prevent an ill-disposed person from cheating.

Out of doors in target archery there will be a maximum of four archers to each target under FITA rules, while six archers per target is permissible for the traditional competitive shooting in the United Kingdom. For indoor contests on smaller target faces the maximum would be four.

Competitions involve the shooting of certain numbers of arrows at each of a number of different distances, shot in decreasing order. Each of these

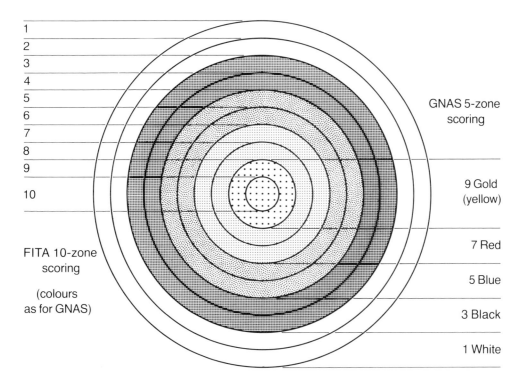

Target archery target faces

combinations of numbers of arrows and distances is known as a 'round'.

For example, the FITA Outdoor Target Round, the basis of international competition in target archery, calls for the shooting of 36 arrows at each of four different distances: for men 90, 70, 50 and 30m and for women 70, 60, 50 and 30m. In the United Kingdom the long established rounds for major contests are known as the York Round (for men) and the Hereford Round (for women); in each of these rounds 72 arrows are shot at the longest of the three distances, 48 at the next and 24 at the shortest. For men the distances are 100, 80 and 60yd and for women 80, 60 and 50yd.

Many other rounds are listed for the GNAS handicap and classification schemes, those requiring fewer arrows to be shot proving invaluable for halfday events where there can be more emphasis on the social aspects of the competition. Except in major international events where the FITA round is shot over two days, the FITA, York and Hereford rounds are very much whole day affairs, starting early in the day and going on until late afternoon or early evening.

Now work is in hand to generate more spectator interest in the international scene and to make the shooting more exciting for television coverage. At major international championships a system of eliminations in a short series of halfday contests leading to a grand final in which only eight men and eight women compete for the title has been devised and is today in use in many countries.

All this is far removed from competition in the archer's club. The new archer has to know how to record scores and conduct himself so that he and his fellow archers can enjoy their competition to the full. Once he has committed himself to club membership one of his first purchases must be a copy of his national archery association's rules of shooting – that is, if his club does not present him with a copy when he joins. This is dry-as-dust reading out of the context of actual shooting, so it will help to describe what happens when a club has one of its regular competition days.

Competition in the club

Most club programmes include a wide variety of shoots, even where it is possible only to accommodate target archery, so that the club can cater for all tastes and levels of experience. Procedures and etiquette encountered in the club should be identical with those at a tournament, albeit on a smaller scale. Most clubs can put down permanent markings for their range layout while there should be no shortage of willing hands to set out the targets in readiness for shooting.

In any well organised club, shooting will commence dead on time, one of the members acting as field captain and giving the signals for shooting to begin and for the archers to advance to the targets to collect arrows and record scores.

The routine where GNAS rules of shooting operate is that half the archers will take their positions on the shooting line and each shoot three arrows – as they finish and vacate their places on the line the remaining archers occupy the vacant spaces to shoot three arrows. This process continues with the first detail returning to the shooting line to shoot a second three arrows, followed in turn by the second detail.

When everybody has shot, the field captain gives the signal for the archers to advance. It is important that archers keep their eyes open as they advance so that they can avoid stepping on or walking into any arrows that have fallen short. It is a tradition, originating in the days when only wooden arrows were in use, that if anyone damaged an arrow in this way he paid for it in cash on the spot. Arrows are not cheap, so it pays to be careful in this situation. Where arrows have fallen in front of the target the owners should note where they fell and remove them before scoring takes place lest they suffer damage.

The first end of six arrows is a 'sighter' end and is not scored. Its purpose is to allow the archers to adapt to the environment – weather, atmosphere, company and surroundings – before the contest begins in earnest and to enable them to set their sights more precisely for the first distance of the tournament.

The next end will be the first scoring end and the routine set out above will again be followed. In a club there will not be any independent non-shooting scorers, neither will there be any such at any tournament in the United Kingdom unless it be a World or European championship event. For anything less it has proved impossible to attract volunteers in sufficient numbers. The GNAS rules provide that one archer on each target shall be target captain. This archer will be responsible for the orderly conduct of shooting on his target and for ensuring that all scores on his target are correctly recorded, even though the actual entry of the scores on the score sheet is delegated to another archer. A second archer on that target will act as lieutenant, his function being to assist the target captain and to identify the arrows in the target with the scores called by the archers. Target captains and lieutenants have a joint responsibility for ensuring that all entries and totals on the score sheets are correct.

Sadly, many archers are averse to being involved with the simple arithmetic needed for totalling the scores, and at tournaments it has been known for prizes to be wrongly awarded because the scores have been incorrectly added. This even though both target captain and archers have signed the score sheet to certify its correctness.

When scoring, neither the arrows nor the target face shall be touched by anybody, not even the judge, until all arrows have been scored and the target captain has given permission for the arrows to be withdrawn. The procedure is for each archer in turn to point to his arrows and call the values of the

Archers at the targets calling and recording their scores (1987 UK Masters Tournament)

scoring zones in which they have landed, starting with the highest value and continuing in descending order. To make life easier for the target captain it is good form to call the scores in groups of three, for example; 'nine, seven, seven (pause) five, three, miss'. It is easier and better to be formal and say 'miss' rather than to be casual and say 'one away' or 'one in the green', which can be misheard and recorded as 'one' instead of the miss it should be. A good target captain will repeat the scores as he writes them down so that all can hear.

Many slipshod habits originate in the club and these can lead to unnecessary irritations at tournaments. Chief among these is the habit adopted by many archers of looking at their arrows, noting their values in their personal score books and reading from them when asked to call their scores. Target captains worth their salt soon put a stop to this but human nature is such that it often falls to one of the judges at a tournament to intervene so that scoring is conducted properly.

Although not provided for in GNAS rules of shooting for target archery the practice of having two separate scorers for each target has much to commend it. Both enter the values of the arrows called by the archers and compare them before the arrows are withdrawn. Totalling the scores is also done independently before the totals are compared. The other archers keep an eye on the values of the arrows belonging to the scorers.

Sometimes an arrow lands so that while in one scoring zone it appears to touch the dividing line with the next higher zone. In most cases it is quite clearly touching or cutting the higher zone but sometimes it can seem to be

74

just outside and there may be differences of opinion. If the target captain cannot give a decision acceptable to the archers he will have to call the judge for a ruling. In the club the decision is usually made quickly and acceptably without recourse to the field captain but at a tournament, especially where the competitor is likely to be a strong contestant for the leadership, much may depend upon the decision and the judge's approach can in no way be a casual one. Judges are trained to give rapid and firm decisions on the values of such borderline arrows; when they themselves cannot be sure they will decide in the archer's favour. Good judges will be positive in their pronouncements; 'that is a five' or 'score seven, please' will leave no one in any doubt about the decision.

Scorers can make mistakes in entering the values of arrows and if the mistake is discovered before any arrows are withdrawn something can be done to rectify it. Here the judge is called to make and initial the necessary correction – it is a good idea to get used to this in the club and to call the field captain to do the job rather than lightly dismiss the alteration as 'one of those things'.

Finally, after all the scores have been recorded and arrows withdrawn, the archers look in the ground for any arrows that have not already been picked up. Sometimes the arrow will be completely buried in the grass – it is good form for *all* the archers on that target to help look for it, though if the search is taking too long the judge or field captain will ask them to search again next time they advance to score and suggest that the archer uses a spare arrow for the time being. This is where a metal detector is useful, but only if the operator systematically sweeps across the target area from side to side and not haphazardly up and down.

In the club it is usually easier to move the targets on completion of the first distance. Shooting at the second distance will normally continue as soon as the targets have been moved and resecured, unless the change coincides with the time of a break for refreshment. There will be no sighters at the second or subsequent distances shot on the same day.

At the end of the day's shooting the highest priority will be to unrig targets and other field equipment and return them to the club store. For this all members are expected to lend a hand. The club records officer collects the score sheets as soon as the final totals have been entered and agreed – results can wait then until the archers have packed up their bows, arrows and other equipment. Unless a member has an unusually pressing engagement it is good manners to remain on the ground until the results of the day's shooting have been announced. Very likely – if the club has the facilities – most club members will stay on for a social gathering with tea or light refreshments. Alternatively the members may gather at a nearby cafe or hostelry. Any informal gathering of members after a day's shooting is worthwhile as a means of strengthening the club bonds.

Competition at tournaments

Club competition is ideal basic training for future competition at tournaments, particularly if the club makes an occasion out of each internal contest. Here the archer will be shooting only with people he already knows.

At a tournament he will be among strangers, often from places quite distant from his club. When tournament organisers make the draw to assign competitors to the various targets they set out to arrange as far as possible that no two archers from any one club are on the same target. For example, a group of six archers from club A may find themselves dispersed among targets numbered 8 to 13 inclusive. In this way even at a comparatively small local tournament the emerging beginner will find himself without the immediate contact and support of his friends. Knowing this he can better prepare himself for his first tournament.

Preparation for the first tournament

Preparation for any tournament begins days before the due date. Entry forms and fees have been sent in long since and in all probability the target list, travel directions and other essential information will be to hand. The priority now is the equipment. It is often taken for granted that, because the archer's bow, arrows and accessories have been used regularly, they will be in good shape – but this should never be left to chance. A thorough check well in advance will boost the archer's morale because he then *knows* that he has taken trouble over his tackle and has done everything possible to avoid equipment failure on the day of the competition.

If he has at least one spare bowstring already shot in and identical in every respect with the one he is currently using; if he has a minimum of two spare arrows to exactly the same specification as those he intends to use; if he is sure that all nuts, screws and other fastenings on his bow sight, handle section and stabilisers are free from damage, a good fit and do not shake loose with the first arrow he looses, then he is not only very well prepared for his first entry into tournament competition but also is paving the way for future contests.

The first tournament – on the day

Anticipation is far worse than the event itself. The newcomer to archery will succumb to stage fright to some extent, and who would blame him? Nevertheless some things can be done to take the sting out of the situation.

In the first place there will be an element of excitement so it will help to preface the event with an early night or two, especially if it is necessary to set out for the shoot at the crack of dawn. If an early start is essential then all necessary items should have been assembled the previous day: bow, arrows, accessories, spares, waterproofs, extra sweater – whatever is thought suitable for the occasion. It is handy to have a check list and to use it every time, for

Shelter for competitors. At a domestic event the archers bring their own – something more to be carried!

many an archer's enjoyment has been spoiled because he forgot little things like tab or bracer.

Travel directions are indispensable; if heading for unfamiliar territory extra time should be allowed for occasionally losing the way. A reasonable objective is to arrive at the tournament field at least ¾hr before the scheduled assembly time. This may seem a long while, but by the time the archer has reported his arrival to the organisers, located the position of the target he has been assigned to, unpacked and assembled his equipment ready to shoot he will find he has barely time to have a cup of coffee before the whistle is blown for assembly.

Assembly is the occasion for calling all the competitors together so that they can be welcomed by the organisers. This is also the time to introduce any local dignitaries present – the mayor, perhaps, welcoming visitors and declaring the event open. Then comes the introduction of the archery officials: the lady paramount and the judges. In the United Kingdom the lady paramount has the honour of being supreme arbitrator should any matter not be resolved by the judges. The lady paramount also has the better known function of presenting the prizes at the end of the tournament.

Introductions over and the tournament formally opened, the organiser gives out general notices such as the location of amenities, availability of refreshments and any special features, and then hands control over to the judges. These would advise the archers of any special procedures required or of any recent rule changes that might not yet be wholly familiar. The last announcement before the archers disperse to their positions is usually the warning that shooting will commence in so many minutes.

Shooting begins and continues very much as in the well organised club but will take a little longer because there are more archers and because more archers will be taking greater care with their shooting. However archers who take too long over shooting three arrows (ie longer than 2½min) will risk the wrath of the judges – when a FITA round is being shot under time control each detail shoots separately and arrows shot outside the permitted time will not score.

Any archer used to shooting in a club and attending a tournament for the first time will miss his friends' light-hearted banter. On the other hand he has stepped into the wider world of the sport and has the chance to meet and talk with archers from other places. After that he is unlikely to return to the closed community of the club to the exclusion of all further tournament shooting.

What happens at changes of distance will depend upon the organiser's arrangements – at an all-day event the lunch break will come at the halfway point. Over the years it has been the practice in the United Kingdom to

Moving targets at change of distance. One archer lifts stand and boss, taking the load on his back, while a second archer lifts and pushes the back leg of the stand

An efficient field party contributes greatly to the success of a tournament. Here the field party fixes 80cm faces to bosses preparatory to shooting at 50m in the FITA Round

move the targets when shooting the FITA outdoor target round and to move the shooting line when shooting other rounds but today it is more common to keep a constant shooting line and move the targets irrespective of the round being shot, the competitors helping to move the targets while the organiser's field party lines them up in position and secures them against being blown over by the wind. The process has speeded up considerably as archers have become more accustomed to this practice and more willing to assist. They now recognise that it is in their own interests to have the targets moved and set up quickly and efficiently.

At the end of the day when shooting has ended there will be a waiting period before the results can be announced. If awards are made only to the outright winners, men and women separately, and to the runners-up then little time will be required for the scores-room party to produce the results. In most cases there will be various awards – by handicap or classification, for married couples, for county members and visitors separately, for club or county teams and possibly some novelty awards. All these extras take time if

79

they are to be sorted accurately, so there may be a wait of up to an hour after the end of shooting before the prizegiving begins.

The problem for both archers and tournament organisers is how to fill in this waiting time. So much depends upon local facilities – at some venues there will be both shelter and refreshments available while at others there may be nothing. A few clubs have put on a novelty shoot for a few ends, sometimes on a knockout basis, to help fill the gap. More frequently there is a raffle, the draw for which precedes the prizegiving. Even that cannot begin too soon after the end of shooting because the archers will be dismantling their equipment and packing it into their vehicles for the homeward journey. Meanwhile the organisers must have their helpers clearing the field – not such a rush if it is their own shooting ground though everyone has a home to go to and no doubt a meal awaiting them when they eventually get there.

There is often complaint about the apparent discourtesy of archers who do not remain on the field for the prizegiving. If the weather has been unkind and they have finished the shoot cold and wet thoughts of possible prizes are probably the last to enter their minds, the more so if they have a long crosscountry journey before reaching home. Nevertheless, where several archers from the same or neighbouring clubs attend a tournament it should be possible to arrange for at least one to stay – it can save the organisers a lot of trouble and expense in posting a sometimes fragile package. Sometimes the prize is a valuable challenge trophy – sensible organisers always have the archer sign for it, undertaking to return it in good condition for the same event the following year. It is a tragedy when such trophies get lost as has been known to happen.

On return home the archer may be weary as well as hungry – in most cases he has warmed up and dried out during the journey home. Food and bed are priority items in his thoughts. But stop! There is something else; the equipment – before it is put away – should be cleaned and dried while arrows that have become bent, lost nocks or fletchings, should be set aside for early attention as should any other item needing maintenance or repair. Good archers are meticulous in caring for their tackle.

After the first tournament
The archer will be eagerly awaiting the arrival of the results – he will want to know how his performance compared with that of fellow club members, and then he will want to know how he fared overall. Even more important, though he may not be aware of it, is whether he shot better or worse under competition conditions than at the club. Tradition has it that competition scores tend to be lower than those shot at the club but there is no good reason for this if the archer has properly prepared himself. In fact a well prepared archer might be expected to return better scores in competition as a result of shooting in a more disciplined environment.

A tournament shooting line. Junior targets are placed between the adult women's and men's targets to integrate them into the event. The disabled archer is competing on equal terms with the able-bodied men

What he will have seen at the tournament is the equipment and accessories that other competitors bring with them. Bought at one and the same time the aggregate cost could be astronomical so he must list his priorities, deciding for himself what is immediately essential for the next competition and what could be left for another time. He should not be unduly influenced by what the next person uses; what that person regards as essential could well be dismissed by another as a mere frill. An important consideration must always be weight and bulk of equipment – after all the archer has to carry all his gear at some stage and it can sometimes be a long walk from car park to shooting field. Although not proven, it is suspected that more archers suffer injury as a direct result of carrying equipment than from any other archery-related cause.

This first tournament may have influenced the archer in another way. He will have seen archers shooting with personal styles quite different from those seen at his club and quite different from the way his coach has taught him. These same archers may have shot far higher scores so an understandably human reaction would be to copy them slavishly – the temptation is great indeed. Nevertheless such slavish copying would be a serious error. The new archer would be well advised to discuss what he has seen with his coach. Probably some of the archers he has seen have never had the benefit of formal coaching beyond essential early instruction in how to shoot safely – they have developed their performance entirely unaided and have succeeded to a high degree in reproducing exactly, shot after shot, their own personal way of shooting, regardless of inbuilt structural defects. Just think of how much better they might have been had they achieved the same degree of exact repetition and applied the same dedication and determination when using their body structure more efficiently and with less unnecessary tension. This is not to say that archers should all be cast in the same mould – that would be every bit as bad as if all traces of individuality were to be taken from them.

The best advice the coach can give the archer when discussing that first tournament and the shooting techniques of other more successful archers is, that he should continue on the path set out for him by his coach, putting in the time and effort towards refining the shooting form he is already developing. The quest is for perfection in shooting, which will automatically bring good scores, and not just for high scores regardless of how they are achieved.

CHAPTER SEVEN

Working for improvement

After his first tournament the archer will have the idea that he is not shooting as well as many others (or rather, is not achieving the same level of scores – which is quite a different thing). He will probably resolve to spend more time at the club to practise to a greater extent than formerly, thinking that the time and effort will pay off handsomely.

Unfortunately this is rarely the case; he will be shooting on his own or in company with fellow archers who will be equally wrapped up in their own shooting and problems associated with it. He is like a traveller setting out without map or compass and with no great sense of direction, often ending up at his original starting point having travelled in a circle.

The suggestion has been made that such an archer should go to his shooting ground taking all his equipment *but only one arrow,* On arrival he would set up all his equipment and then sit down and carefully think through everything his coach has ever told him about the sequence of shooting an arrow, of how he should use his body and manipulate his bow and arrow. That done he would go to the shooting line taking every care with positioning, preparation and the actions that follow. All this leads up to the steady and deliberate shooting of the single arrow he has taken with him.

The arrow shot and collected, the archer again sits down, thinks through the shot he has just made – and then packs up his tackle, taking the same care in putting it away as in setting it out. After all this he returns home.

Ridiculous? It sounds so, but in the absence of a coach the archer has probably gained a benefit infinitely greater than would result from shooting several dozen arrows with his clubmates. The reason; the whole exercise has been planned, the archer is working to a set programme and is subjecting himself to a far more rigorous discipline than he would encounter elsewhere. If he can see it through in the true spirit of the exercise as well as to the letter and can subsequently repeat it with the same integrity he will have achieved a level of control over both self and bow that will remain with him throughout his archery career.

Above all this gives point to the truth that, no matter when or where, there is only one important arrow. This is the arrow the archer is preparing to shoot. All previous arrows are beyond recall and thus of no account. All future arrows are still in the future because they are not the arrow the archer has in his bow. The archer's sole concern must be with the present.

Few archers would have the courage to attempt this single arrow task — fear of failure or of the temptation to shoot that one arrow a second, third, fourth or more times is too great.

Controlled practice

Controlled practice is setting out to shoot with a specific objective in mind. Such objectives are many and varied, depending on the needs of the archer. They need to be initiated by a coach so that the archer can familiarise himself with the task before proceeding to work at it on his own.

Practice within the club often ends up with shooting arrows for a certain time with no clearly defined objective — and it shows! Just look at any collection of archers at a tournament.

In his formative years, controlled practice means the substitution of good habits for bad; the refinement of imperfectly developed stages in the sequence of shooting, working to achieve mastery of the bow at all times in an activity where the forces exerted on the archer by the drawn bow can so easily run away with the unwary; building in degrees of motivation undreamed of by the novice; enhancing adaptability to climate and environment and the development of endurance so that at the end of a day's shooting in adverse conditions the archer has maintained his shooting form with strength and energy left to enable him to continue shooting in like form if need be.

Good habits for bad

At one time it was commonplace to speak of an archer's 'faults' and to be specific over what was wrong with his way of shooting (usually indicating symptom rather than cause) without saying what was right or what could be done to remedy the situation — but not any more.

Today more is known about how bad habits can subtly enter into an archer's way of shooting and of the way in which an archer *thinks* he is doing things compared with *how* he actually does them. Many troubles stem from the visually orientated approach that western life and culture engender. Archers depend far too little upon their sense of touch and upon their awareness of what parts of their body are functioning as they stand, prepare to shoot, bring the bow to full draw and take the shot through the loose into the follow through.

Most common among the bad habits prevalent today is that of taking short cuts, merging two or three of the stages in the shooting sequence into a single more complex action. Even without the presence of a coach the archer can do much to help himself by returning to first principles and developing each shot, step by step, as outlined in Chapters 4 and 5. The real danger arising from taking short cuts is that the archer does not give himself a chance to put his body in the best position for drawing the bow. Consequences vary from hunched shoulders, an apparently high front shoulder (in reality a low front arm) to excessive body movement in which the archer attempts to use his body weight to draw the bow instead of bringing shoulder and back muscles into play.

From the point of view of the coach the replacement of bad habits by good is an uphill task unless the archer is completely willing to put the effort into the task and will admit to himself that he needs to go back to basics. It takes courage to admit that this is what is needed.

There is no effect without cause so why do these bad habits creep in? Absence of a coach cannot stand up as a real reason. Today archers at least pay lip service to the idea of a sequence of actions in the making of a shot, even if they do not put it into practice so well. One contributory factor is the mass of the present day bow with its metal handle and array of stabilisers – the effort to lift it and hold it at arm's length is considerable compared with that required for a simple unadorned bow. So, if the archer is to work on sequence and position, it would pay handsomely to shed unnecessary loading and completely remove the stabiliser array while developing a new sense of position and sequence or – more likely – relearning something learned previously and unconsciously abandoned. Let him master that and then gradually increase the loading until he is in full control with his normal array of stabilisers.

A more likely opening for the formation of bad habits is haste. Archers shooting on a club target day tend to be over-ambitious, even to the extent of shooting or attempting to shoot a York round in a morning! In the long run this harms both club and archers. The pace of shooting at a club target day should differ very little from that at an open tournament. Since the maximum permitted time for the shooting of three arrows is 2½min and since most archers will have shot three arrows in less than 1½min under normal conditions there is absolutely no need for haste. Every action in archery, especially the preparation for the shot, must be deliberate and fully under control so that the archer can stop at any stage in the sequence and return to the starting point should he sense that something is not quite right.

Other casualties resulting from haste are attention to detail and precision. Archers today must pay attention to detail in preparing to make the shot if they are to be regarded as marksmen. That fraction of a second extra to ensure that the action is properly executed is time well spent. Precision in handling the equipment is equally important. Remember the comparisons with guns in an earlier chapter – near enough is not good enough if the archer wishes himself to be considered as a marksman rather than as someone just playing with bows and arrows.

Haste is the culprit, too, in misuse of the body when drawing the bow. Many archers almost literally 'fling themselves' into the action of drawing the bow. Instead of working from a previously prepared standing position, where bodily alignment is of the utmost importance, the hurried draw becomes a convulsion wherein brute force is substituted for skill, very much like the effect of taking short cuts mentioned earlier.

Haste shows itself in other ways – impatience to achieve results, for example. The outside world today displays so many 'instant' technical achievements that the unsuspecting archer is conditioned to expect instant enhancement of scoring potential by adapting the latest applications of technology to archery equipment. Similarly he expects instantaneous improvement at any coaching clinic he attends or from any consultation with the coach in his own club. With such expectations the archer is doomed to disappointment – application of coaching to replacement of bad habits with good is rarely rapid, while – and not decrying the technological developments – even the less highly specified equipment today has a far greater potential for delivering good shots than has the archer using it. Remember that top of the range equipment is often less forgiving of the archer's errors and may well magnify them to his lasting dismay. So it is necessary to return all the time to the universal guiding principle 'one thing at a time', whether considering the archer's shooting or his tackle.

One change is introduced, the one thing that in the long run will effect the greatest overall improvement, and then consolidated. When, and only when, this consolidation is complete will it be time enough for the coach to consider the next most necessary and beneficial change in the archer's shooting form.

Refinement

While an archer can fairly quickly develop a superficially acceptable way of shooting in the club environment there will still be many variables not under the archer's full control.

Refinement exists in working with the coach to identify sources of variation, to assess priorities in the refinement programme of training and to work with patience and perseverance. Even more important, refinement exists in identifying what the archer has already achieved with some success and enhancing the already good features of his shooting so that they become even better. Again there will be areas of priority and a training programme to be devised for the archer.

While all this is going on, the archer is steadily increasing his resistance to the forces exerted on him by the drawn bow. He appreciates far more than in his novice days the benefit of transferring as much as possible of the load of the drawn bow from muscles to bone structure and he has worked towards achieving this, albeit not without some prompting from the coach. It is all too easy to concentrate upon one aspect – the immediate job in hand – and unknowingly slacken off in other respects.

Shooting in competition needs automatic responses to the environment, to changes in force and direction of wind and to the feel of the drawn bow. The archer who ponders over every detail of every shot that he makes will do this at the expense of concentration on the target and to the exclusion of extraneous distractions. As well as a sequence there is a rhythm in the act of shooting – not a rhythm that is unyielding and unvarying in its application to the shooting of an arrow but one that is responsive to subtle changes of atmosphere around the archer so that he remains calm and master of his bow at all times. A good archer will be aware of these things without need for them to intrude into conscious thought.

Competition in archery is unlike any other form of competition – there is no interaction with any opponent. The opponent is the archer himself so the action is completely self-contained. There is no competitor obviously in front as in running and, except for major tournaments where a leader board displays interim results, there will be no indication of position in order of scores made until after the event.

Working for mastery of the bow

It is for this reason that the competitive archer needs to develop a very strict mental discipline.

Many coaches think of the competitor's year in three parts:

a) rest and relaxation immediately following the end of the competitive season with physical activity (of a non-damaging kind) taken in a form well removed from archery;

b) preparation and training for the next season of competition with further development of all the attributes needed for good shooting and the commissioning and working up of all new items of equipment;

c) the competitive season during which training is limited to the maintenance of fitness, stamina and existing shooting form.

Rest and relaxation

Competitive seasons differ and overlap, depending upon the particular discipline in archery that the archer follows. In the United Kingdom the outdoor target archery season runs from April to October, with the field archery season extending further into the winter months. Indoor target archery events are commonly set from November to April.

Some competitors are equally at home in more than one of these main disciplines, sometimes taking in all three – they, more than most others, are aware of the fundamental similarities and differences and can more readily adapt when they cross the boundary.

A number of archers find the change of discipline itself a relaxation, or use one as a form of rest from another. For some high level competitors, rest and relaxation will come with a complete abandonment of archery for some weeks – the equivalent of taking a holiday. This does not mean a complete letting go of all physical activity – dancing (of a kind calling for a certain amount of skill rather than its pursuit in the alcohol- and tobacco-laden atmosphere of a disco), swimming, walking or cycling all help to maintain good body tone and at the same time in themselves all are enjoyable both as gentle relaxation and as tasks in which the individual can push himself to the limit of his capabilities. The important thing is not to let go completely but to maintain that level of fitness and flexibility that allows an easy transition into preparing for the coming competitive season.

Preparation training
It is hoped that this will include the application of those lessons learned during the previous season. This is a period of self-analysis, looking at the potential goals, the likelihood of attaining them and the means by which they might be attained. This is also a time for very close co-operation between archer and coach where the latter listens seriously to the archer thinking aloud and looks at ways in which the archer's performance can be strengthened and for variables that ought to be made less so. Both archer and coach must be aware of the dangers of setting goals so remote that the archer thinks of them as impossible or so trivial that they are passed without serious effort. Round figures as objectives in scoring are to be avoided – missing a target figure of 1,121 in a FITA Outdoor Target Round by just a few points can still produce a score of over 1,100, yet it is common for an archer to have an objective of 1,100 and end up with 1,092 or thereabouts. The performance of the previous year is more a yardstick of what can be done and hopefully surpassed than a starting point for the current year.

The recently (1985) introduced FITA Finals Round produces a situation in which every arrow counts and scotches for all time the thought 'I can make up for those bad arrows in the next end, dozen, distance, or on the second, third or fourth day'. It is easy to believe but in practice it creates tension, breaks concentration, is a procrastination and seldom (if ever) does it work.

The beauty of the nine arrows at each distance, first in descending order of distance and then in ascending order is that flexibility and adaptability are encouraged in the training sessions. If training is well done in this area then the FITA Outdoor Target Round, or the York and Hereford Rounds will hold fewer terrors apart from those of repetition and (for some) boredom.

In one of the earlier trials of the FITA Finals Round the average scores for each set of 36 arrows decreased from set to set throughout the round. The objective for both archer and coach must be to reverse this trend.

Other things apart from shooting are essential to the preparation programme. Fitness, flexibility and strength each have their place. Precise control of the drawn bow, essential for good marksmanship in archery, requires that the archer be in good health so that in major competition he can continue through several days of shooting without fatigue taking its toll. Mobility of the joints in arms and shoulders and around the hips and lower spine is also fundamental for fine and precise control.

Everyone must have encountered stiff or corroded hinges or a sticking drawer – there is resistance to all attempts to move them until greater effort is applied at which the resistance is overcome and the movement is both sudden and unexpected and often much more than is desired. Stiffness in the arms and shoulders or at the hips, due to lack of exercise (as distinct from any specific medical condition), results in action that is explosive and lacking control.

Weight training has been the subject of much controversy. In archery there is no need for great strength or for vast muscle development – too much muscle can get in the way. Likewise there is no call for explosive effort, for what the archer needs all through the process of shooting an arrow is control. It follows that any exercises with weights should be with light weights only while the exercises should be devised so that the archer ends up being better able to exercise control while drawing, aiming and taking the shot through into the follow through. Care is necessary also to see that such training complements the established need for good posture.

Part of the application of weight training is psychological – it induces a feeling of well being, a sense of having done something extra, of being one step ahead of the opposition. This is why it is best for the keen competitive archer not to go it alone but to consult those who are experts in the application of weight training to seemingly unrelated physical activity. Incorrect application of weight training is likely to impair rather than enhance performance in archery, so such training should only be undertaken under expert supervision.

It is good for the archer to continue as far as time will allow those alternative physical activities he took up during the rest and relaxation months.

Preparation – the equipment
This is the time, too, to buy replacement equipment and to check carefully that destined to be used for at least one further season. Anything new needs to be 'run in'; it must get used to the archer every bit as much as the archer must get used to the new item. This includes spares of whatever kind. Even if they are intended to be identical to what is already in use it pays to leave nothing to chance. In this area bowstrings more than anything else have priority – strings made of kevlar have a strictly limited life and 'high mileage' strings should be discarded even if they still look good for at least

another round. A broken bowstring is something an experienced archer should take in his stride – but why take such a gamble? A breakage disturbs the rhythm of shooting, it can hold up the tournament, it can upset neighbouring archers on the line while the unexpectedness of it cannot but be upsetting to the archer as is the embarrassment of standing up on the line quite alone to shoot the remaining arrows of that end while the Director of Shooting announces 'we have an equipment failure'.

The life expectancies of kevlar strings has been quoted as ranging from 1,000 to 2,000 arrows. Assuming 1,500 to be a reasonable compromise, it will pay to look at these 1,500 arrows. Once made, each string has to be shot in – say for 100 arrows. This leaves 1,400 arrows for tournaments and practice. A FITA Outdoor Target, York or Hereford Round will call for 150 arrows including sighters and typically a two day event will be a double round or 300 arrows. Four such weekends of double rounds account for 1,200 arrows, leaving only 200 for training purposes.

Using these figures as a guide, the archer can soon calculate the number of strings he needs to make each season so that he has more than sufficient to ensure that he does not run out at a critical point. 'Unused' strings will keep for the following season. At this rate of use the archer will need to be methodical and should number each string and keep an accurate log of the arrows shot with it so that he can pension it off at the end of its expected life.

During this preparation period it helps to make spare strings in batches – not everybody has a spare room or workshop where jigs and materials are always to hand. Not only will there be a sense of rhythm in the task but also production can be planned to make the best use of available time.

Every archer has his own favourite shooting tab – it has become an old and trusted friend – but even the best of tabs does not last for ever. It pays to have one or two spares of the same kind already shot in and ready for use. By doing so there will be confidence that the change from old to new will have no effect on shooting form.

Arrows take a lot of punishment during their lifetime – shock of discharge, initial flexing, impact with the target or nearby objects, vibrations after impact and, from time to time, strikes on shaft or nock from other arrows. As time goes by small imperfections creep in – a hurried refletching might affect the flight of the shaft – careless handling, perhaps by a fellow archer, could introduce a minute bend.

For novice or recreational archer this might not matter too much but the competitive archer leaves nothing to chance; he always takes more than enough arrows with him so that it would be an evil day indeed if he ran out of spares. At the beginning of each season the competitor will check every single arrow and set aside any that are less than perfect for use in high risk situations (clout, roving, field archery – in the case of the target archer using this as a diversion – or for loan to a new archer who wishes to sample arrows of different specifications before making a purchase). Then he will restock to the identical specification that he knows will suit him and his bow. This is not quite enough for it is not wise to take things too much for granted. Old and new shafts should be shot to see whether they group together satisfactorily.

By doing these things, paying attention to detail, the competitive archer will have that extra confidence in his equipment, knowing that it is just right for him, and thus be able to put it to the back of his mind and leave the field clear for concentration on marksmanship.

The competitive season

When this comes round the archer should be ready. He will have looked through tournament diaries in magazines and newsletters to see what events are being held and where. Most major events in the United Kingdom are arranged for the same weekend year after year so it is possible for the archer to plan his competitive programme for the greater part of the season. For one who has sights set on becoming a member of the national team, be it indoor, outdoor or field, it will be necessary to return as many scores as possible from comparable events shot in open competition. This will govern the number of tournaments at other levels in which he can shoot for pure pleasure.

During preparation training it is difficult for the archer to train to be adaptable to the weather he is most likely to encounter during the competitive season. Preparation in winter and early spring means becoming acclimatised to almost anything that can happen – rain, snow, frost, gales, fog. The competitive archer has suitable clothing to meet these conditions and he knows he can survive and return acceptable scores despite the weather. There is a strong element of challenge in this aspect of preparation.

In the sheltered environment of a sports hall it will never be quite the same – true, working with the coach in sheltered surroundings can iron out variables, ease tensions and make for more effective shooting but in the end the archer will have to take his shooting out of doors for that is where most competition is.

As the competitive season gets into its stride the likelihood of dry, sunny days and higher temperatures increases, although British weather is much less predictable than that in the middle of a continental land mass. The competitor from the United Kingdom, used to frequent combat with the elements, is badly prepared for prolonged hot weather with temperatures of 30°C (86°F) or higher. At the other end of the scale competitors from nations where a prolonged hot dry season is commonplace may end up in a state of near hypothermia if competing in less predictable Northern Europe.

The most unsettling extremes are low temperatures plus heavy rain plus strong winds or high temperatures plus high humidity plus a complete absence of wind.

91

The organisers of the competition and the supporters of the competitors jointly have a responsibility here. For the organisers, the responsibility is first and foremost that of shelter – not so much during the competition whether in almost arctic or in almost tropical conditions – but in the time before the competition begins, in the intervals and after the competition ends; this in the form of shelter from wind and rain or from direct heat of the sun. The next responsibility of the organisers is to make hot drinks (tea, coffee, chocolate, soup) available or cool and preferably still, rather than fizzy, natural drinks. Adequate toilet facilities are essential under any conditions.

The responsibility of the supporters is much more personal – they can look after the personal needs of the individual competitors, fetching and carrying, providing food and drink on demand – erecting individual shelters behind the tent line – ensuring that dry towels are to hand so that rainsodden gear can be handled better – providing additional warm clothing while the archer is waiting – doling out anything that adds to the well being of the competitor, be it sugar, salt tablets or sunburn lotion.

In the end, in spite of all that organisers and supporters can do, the competitive archer must do his own homework on the likely environment he could encounter in travelling to other parts of his own country or when travelling abroad, anticipating his needs by deduction where he cannot gain firsthand experience beforehand and seeking the best possible advice from coaches, team managers and fellow archers who have already been to similar places.

This emphasis on climate is deliberate because so many competitors are not well prepared for environmental changes, even today. True, they have the right clothing and accessories and can shoot adequately – but are they mentally attuned to such changes? Too many will talk themselves into a state of panicky collapse because they complain so much about the cold, the wet, the wind, the heat and the humidity.

They forget that it is the same for everyone on the field. In complaining they are indulging in negative thinking of the worst kind.

Rather they should be congratulating themselves that they had the foresight to don their thermal underwear and that their waterproofs are in good shape. Even more, they should be congratulating themselves that in doing their preparation training they have proved to themselves that they can perform well in spite of the elements.

Likewise with the other extreme; they spend half the year eagerly looking forward to the summer – so if the summer should turn out to be extremely hot and somewhat humid what cause have they for complaint? They can rejoice instead that they have no need for those waterproofs and extra layers of clothing. Being thus unencumbered they have greater freedom of movement where it matters most to an archer – around the upper part of the body –

Culmination of sound preparation. Winning girls at the Junior Championships of Europe and the Mediterranean 1987. (l to r) Natalie Pitel (URS), Jenny Sjowall (SWE) and Claudia Loroff (FRG)

and so, in theory, everything is on their side.

All they have to do is to get up on that shooting line and shoot.

Food for thought

One thing not mentioned so far is food. It does not immediately relate to shooting but nevertheless it has a place in the routine of a competitive archer. In his own country there is usually no problem. A normal diet generally will suffice. There is so much attention paid today to healthy eating that one begins to wonder whether it is safe to eat at all. Moderation in all things is a realistic guideline.

Abroad it may be quite different – different raw materials, ways of preparing food, service, standards of hygiene and even quantities. In the larger hotels cuisine is generally more international and will differ less from country to country than will local and traditional ways of eating. Food in the larger hotels is often much richer than at home while the menu in some areas could have a much higher proportion and variety of seafood.

The much travelled individual will have some idea of how well his stomach can cope with unfamiliar dishes but the inexperienced traveller will be at a loss. A severe stomach upset does not go well with major competitive activity. Advice can only be in general terms because individual adaptability varies so much.

In some parts of the world water supplies may be imperfect – and while locals are no doubt able to take this in their stride, when in doubt drink bottled mineral water instead of from the tap. Drinks prepared from boiled water – tea, coffee, chocolate – can also be considered safe. A combination of alcohol and very rich food can have unpleasant consequences, so any intake of alcohol should be minimal. Think of how drink has been shown to impair driving a motor vehicle – so what might it do to the precise control needed for high level performance in archery?

Meat pies and cold meats are often suspect, sometimes with justification, although they are commonly staple lunchtime fare at tournaments, especially in packed lunches. Many other things have been suspect from time to time, even salads, so in the end the individual may have little choice but to take what is on offer and hope for the best. It would be unwise to go entirely without food at lunchtime unless such was the established everyday routine of the individual.

The best general advice is that, where a choice is available, the competitor should avoid the exotic – at least until the contest is over – and eat as nearly as possible familiar foods or traditional dishes of the host country.

Some countries specialise in their breakfasts, others in their lunches while elsewhere the evening meal is the focal point of the day's eating. For the competitive archer it is commonsense to have something more than just a cup of tea and a bowl of cereal for breakfast if at all possible – it will be a long time until lunch with much waiting around apart from the shooting – though this advice would be difficult to follow if the hotel only supplies a continental breakfast and strictly rations the quantity per person.

CHAPTER EIGHT

The role of the coach

In the beginning (c1949), organised coaching in British archery was an activity dealing with classes rather than individuals. The requirement was one of teaching the elements of how to shoot safely, after which everyone was left to his own devices to soldier on as best he could.

The problem is that to anyone not involved with the sport the act of shooting, when properly performed, looks easy and effortless. Few laymen appreciate the extent of the physical and mental self-discipline required for the archer to be able to give this impression. Even archers were not then aware of the complexities of the processes they were dealing with and instruction in how to shoot was a matter of personal opinion with little accurate observation or scientific background to justify it.

Since that time much progress has been made in several countries and training for coaches is today based on a broad consensus developed over two or three decades and backed up by expert input from several sources.

The dictionary offers little help towards definition of the role of the coach, merely saying: 'private tutor, instructor of athletics team, etc'. In the broadest sense the coach is like a road map or a sequence of direction signs – he can point out the way, suggest possible alternative routes and attend to breakdowns, but in the end the athlete has to travel the road himself.

The attributes of a coach

The coach is an instructor, not only passing on information on skills and techniques but also ensuring that this information is taken in and put to good use by the archer. The coach is a motivator, encouraging the archer towards his chosen destination and at the same time indicating possible routes. The coach is an organiser and manager, devising programmes appropriate to the training of the archers he is working with and encouraging progress towards agreed and attainable objectives.

The coach is a disciplinarian – not so much for enforcing the very necessary safety procedures and ensuring proper care in using the equipment – for he has to act as the archer's memory until, step by step, the archer is ready to take over. This is a responsibility shared with the athlete for maintaining progress, noting that the coach is aware of the distractions and diversions to which the archer is subject.

The coach is a counsellor. He is interested in the athlete's problems and concerns – who knows how much the athlete's performance will be affected by them if he cannot talk to the coach? Hence the coach must be approachable, a good listener, caring and able to respect any confidences with which he might be entrusted.

The coach is a leader. Politically this can be a dirty word, but lead he must – after all does he not want people to follow him? Is he not leading the archers he trains towards a state of substantial self-sufficiency?

Above all the coach must be a communicator. He must communicate with athletes who are working with him, for if he does not he will be a failure in all his roles as instructor, motivator, organiser, manager, disciplinarian, counsellor and leader – all these depend upon good communication. Never forget that communication is two-way; there must be input to the coach as well as output from him if the coach is to be effective in any of his many roles.

Thus far these attributes are those one would expect of a coach in any sport. What is required of him that is specific to archery? In the first place an insight into the nature of archery – a sport using a simple machine that stores the energy fed into it by the archer drawing the bow and which uses that energy to propel a missile in the direction in which the archer points both himself and the machine (not necessarily the same as the direction in which the archer would like it to point or thinks he is pointing it!).

In some respects the archery coach might have an advantage over coaches in other sporting activities. In contrast to the explosive effort of throwing the hammer or of the run up to a jump the archer is standing still, while his movements to draw the bow are comparatively slow and deliberate. Thus it is possible for an experienced observer to view a succession of shots during which he would note the stages in the sequence, the consistencies and inconsistencies and the structural strengths and weaknesses. True, it is impossible for the human eye to detect the behaviour of the arrow in flight towards the target, but everything that has gone before the release of the string, the placing of the arrows in the target and the movements in the follow through are all there for the trained eye to see and analyse.

On the other hand, while the athlete sets out to jump farther, throw harder or run faster, the requirement in archery is for precision in a series of actions that must be repeated exactly many, many times upon many different days. Thus the coach has to be an accurate observer with a retentive memory, able to retain in his mind the images of previous shots so that he can compare shot with shot – important while the archer is working to develop his technique and is in the process of training himself to be aware of what his body is doing each time as he prepares himself for the shot, draws his bow and takes the shot through release into follow through. The coach has also to be constantly on the alert for signs of unnecessary tension because tensions in the wrong places can undo the work of weeks or months of training.

In the United Kingdom, coaches in archery today are all amateur and usually are fully employed in work that bears no relation to any sporting activity. If archery should ever take off (as it could do with suitable media interest) and grow as golf has done, then there would undoubtedly be a place for the professional. Today with the present population of archers and with current attitudes it is impossible for anyone to earn a living by archery coaching alone. Support in this direction from manufacturers and distributors of archery equipment cannot be expected until there is a firm indication of major growth in the sport.

Coaching as a relationship

If the archer is sufficiently motivated and able to devote the necessary time to his training he will reach the stage where his shooting is technically perfect and structurally strong, and where the observer can honestly say that each shot is an exact repetition of the previous one. The archer, however, may not yet be achieving that exact repetition in the way the shots strike the target.

This is the stage where the role of the coach becomes much more exacting. He has been increasingly relegated to the background as he has helped the archer to achieve self-sufficiency in body awareness and in shooting technique. The archer will be on his own in the competitions for which he is preparing and yet he will want to know how and where he can communicate with his coach. *His* coach, please note – no longer *the* coach. The coach will have taken on a big commitment both in time and money without any hope of reward except that of knowing that he has been instrumental in starting and keeping the archer on the road to success. Self-sufficiency can take some vicious blows on days when nothing seems to go as it should. It is at times like this when the coach becomes a counsellor, a catalyst to set off reactions so that the archer can release his mental tensions, a calming influence so that once the tensions have been released the archer can think over the events of the day, put them in perspective and thrust all negative thoughts behind him.

The positive thinker is the kind of person who says 'my glass is half full' while the negative response would have been 'my glass is half empty'. The trouble is that the negative comes to mind so much more easily than the corresponding positive. So, right from the very beginning of any archer-coach relationship, the coach must take the lead using positive terms, giving positive advice and eschewing all prohibition save where it is essential for health or safety. Negative thinking requires little thought or effort – the totally positive approach calls for much application and reasoned argument.

There is a trap for the archer – he assumes that things should always show

97

signs of improvement or, at worst, should remain the same. If he is unhappy with the scores he is making or with the feel of his shooting he is apt to think that the end of the world is nigh. He will mourn the low scoring arrow and forget all those that were central in the target, he will bewail the few arrows outside his otherwise perfect groups and overlook the fact that for most ends his groups were acceptably tight.

The coach must always take the lead in goal setting. Left to himself the archer tends to be over-ambitious. If the archer habitually shoots FITA rounds of 1,115 to 1,145 in practice the idea of shooting 1,245 in a tournament will be unrealistic. However, if he keeps calm and ignores unsolicited comment, there is no reason why he should not equal his training scores. If the tournament environment duplicates the conditions the archer experienced in training then he could equal or better the scores made in training, but only if he has a strong belief in his own ability. It is one of the tasks of the coach to lead the archer to develop such a belief, a belief that will survive all the battering that competition itself, gamesmanship and well-intentioned but thoughtless approaches from others will impose.

The coach and the beginner

Any coach involved in introducing beginners to archery is in the front line of coaching. This can be a one-to-one relationship or, at the other extreme, a production line job with group after group.

Whatever his task, the ultimate objective is to ensure that the newcomers successfully enjoy their archery. If they do not enjoy it they will not long remain as archers; if they are not successful in it, within the limits of their ability and experience, again they will not long remain as archers.

The prime functions of the coach are, above all, to ensure that the new archer understands all safety procedures to the extent that he can also keep a watchful eye on his peers in this context, can handle the equipment correctly and can use his body effectively, and, with the degree of precision necessary, to make a reasonably good initial showing. The new archer can see for himself how well he can group his arrows and whether there is a gradual but steady improvement from session to session. The coach can increase the degree of difficulty as he sees the need for further challenges for his pupils.

Much enjoyment comes from a successful response to the challenges offered. Even more enjoyment comes from a good social atmosphere in the club, an atmosphere that is difficult though not impossible to generate in a weekly 45min session at a sports centre. In the latter case the personality and enthusiastic approach of the coach to his subject will carry the day.

The coach and the improver

The improver in archery is like the swimmer who has discovered that the initial learning process is at an end and that he can swim without buoyancy

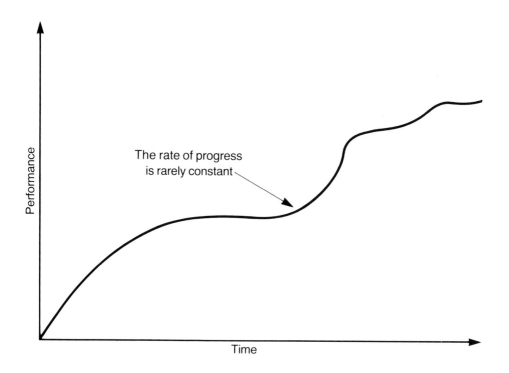

The rate of progress
is rarely constant

Performance

Time

Typical learning curve of beginner

aids. The swimmer has yet to develop the stamina for swimming greater distances at greater speeds and for longer times – he has yet to master the finer points of the various strokes so that he can move more effectively in the water and he has yet to achieve full control of the breathing in time with his strokes. Nevertheless he can swim unaided, something he has never done before. Now he will want to savour the experience before he decides on which direction he would like to develop.

It is much the same for the improver in archery. He feels that he has developed a consistency that gives him some independence from the coach and allows him to shoot alongside other club members. He has decided that he wants to stay in archery and is determined to obtain his own personal equipment at the earliest opportunity.

Here is his first dilemma – he has seen the equipment other club members are using and wants to have something very similar so that he does not stand out from the crowd because he is using something different. A similar dilemma faces the coach; while he wants his protégé to work towards self-sufficiency he knows the improver's limitations and that the over-stabilised bow with a heroic draw weight will often break rather than make

99

the improver. He can foretell that the improver will be yet another person lost to the sport because at this stage he still needs a bow that is relatively light in the hand and with a draw weight that can be handled comfortably throughout a day's shooting.

What the coach wants is the development of a style that looks good to the observer, a straightforward businesslike technique without frills and flourishes where the body is used properly and not ill-treated. At this stage the coach is looking for consistent performance at intermediate distances with a steady rate of development shown by progressively tighter groups and consequential higher scores.

What happens next will depend upon the amount of time the improver really wants to give to his shooting – quite different from the time he could give to it. That initial enthusiasm when he wants to be down at the club every day for two or three hours can easily be killed stone dead, for example, by a prolonged spell of bad weather – the more so if the club has few facilities for shelter.

This is not to say that regular shooting in a fairly intensive programme is a bad thing, but the coach should be present – not breathing down the archer's neck but distant and quietly observing – taking in the overall picture and alert for signs of tension and misuse of the body. At the same time the coach should be giving gentle encouragement and suggesting future goals.

In the matter of personal equipment there must be close consultation between archer and coach. The bow has to suit the archer's present capabilities irrespective of whether it is new or secondhand. Its draw weight must be within the archer's capacity for controlling it from beginning to end of a day's shooting, while its limbs must be long enough to make it a comfortable and forgiving bow to shoot. At the same time the handle must sit nicely in the hand so that placing the hand on the handle can be accurately and comfortably repeated for every shot made.

At this point in his career, the bow and arrows will have a potential for accurate shooting far in excess of anything the improver can achieve, so a middle of the road approach is far more sensible than following the old archers' story of 'the best the archer can afford'. This approach also leaves something in hand for clothing, accessories and for future development. Arrows depend on the choice of bow so their purchase should follow that of the bow.

The coach and the competitive archer

This is coaching as a relationship. Ideally the coach could travel to every tournament with the competitive archer he has helped bring into the sport; in practice this would be unwise. It would be restrictive in terms of the archer's self-sufficiency because, unless the archer is still very dependent, he might find the presence of the coach an implied reflection on his ability to cope with tournament pressure. It is a delicate balance.

Competitive archers come in all degrees of proficiency and many enjoy the competition without ever winning a medal. The minimum condition for the enjoyment of competition at this level is the maintenance of existing form so that scores made are not significantly lower than on any previous occasions. Many competitive archers have variables and weaknesses of one kind or another in their shooting, visible even at fairly high levels of performance. In co-operation with the coach these are capable of being made less variable and of being strengthened, though this takes time to achieve; the golden rule is 'one thing at a time'

Introducing greater consistency into an archer's shooting form and strengthening that form where weaknesses are evident is not synonymous with moulding the individual into a standard pattern. There is no standard pattern but there may be some very close similarities among archers of like physical characteristics. Every archery coach has a mental image of good shooting form but good coaches know that the basic concept of good technique is only a starting point and that the concept has to be tailored to fit the individual archer.

The question so often asked by archers is 'how can I improve my scores?' Scores are only the end product of shooting; unskilled shooting, inconsistent shooting, weak shooting result in low scores. As shooting becomes more skilled, more consistent and with a stronger technique, so the scores will rise. The leading performers, from whatever nation, have worked hard in collaboration with their mentors to develop their skills, to achieve a strong and consistent form.

They have given much thought to what they do so that they instinctively become aware of how their good shots are made and instinctively sense the things that could allow a potentially good shot to become a bad one. They are all very much aware that in a day's tournament they have not shot 150 arrows, but have shot one arrow 150 times or, in other words, have made 150 completely self-contained shots.

So the question put in an earlier paragraph needs to be taken apart and rephrased. If the archer asks 'how can I make a better shot?' there is a strong probability that an answer will be forthcoming. It may not be the answer the archer is secretly longing for. Nobody, archer or coach, has access to a magic formula to transform shooting skill overnight. However, if the archer accepts the answer – namely that the coach has identified inconsistencies, weaknesses or sources of tension – then he will have made the first step in the right direction.

The next thing the archer must accept is that no form, no matter how good, remains absolutely constant. If he can convert all his scores for a variety of rounds into equivalents in terms of the handicap system used in the

United Kingdom, for example, or if he shoots nothing but the FITA Outdoor Target Round in competition then he will see that in either case there will be variations about a mean but all in all a consistent series of values because in that period no changes have been made in the equipment used or in the archer's way of shooting.

So archer and coach agree to work together to iron out variations, strengthen shooting form and eliminate unnecessary tensions.

Now comes something that the coach knows only too well but which most archers have great difficulty in accepting. Whenever a change is made, whether in equipment used or in the archer's way of shooting, there will be a time, often measured in weeks rather than days, during which the archer is becoming used to shooting with the new item or to the modified way of shooting. During this time the level of scores will drop noticeably – this is a fact of life – because the archer will be concentrating on the detail of the shot rather than on the shot itself.

This is particularly the case when there is any change in shooting technique. It may be in the way an archer stands, in the way he places his fingers on the string, in the way he uses his body to store up the energy in the drawn bow. The feel is different, even slightly uncomfortable at first, because the archer has been accustomed to doing things in a certain way for months if not years. It is possible also that he has unconsciously introduced gradual changes himself, changes he might not have intended and that may have proved detrimental to shooting form.

Archers habitually ask 'how can I improve my scores?' What they should be asking is 'am I doing what I think I am doing?', 'am I doing the same thing for every shot that I make?' or 'is there anything I am doing which I could do better if only someone would show me how?' These questions relate directly to what the archer is doing and can be the basis for a good archer-coach relationship. If coach and archer work together to seek out the answers to these questions then better scores will gradually follow. An archer worried about mere numbers will not enjoy his shooting, but an archer working with his coach to answer the more sensible questions will get great pleasure from working towards a specific goal.

How this working together evolves depends upon the personal circum-stances of both archer and coach. Both have to go out of their way to give of their time and effort. Both have to fix dates and times to cover a long period, and both must adhere to these arrangements. Such a degree of commitment cannot be handled casually.

If coach and archer live far from each other, then their meetings have to be at weekends – for a whole day or for the whole weekend – the coach going to the archer or vice versa, according to available shooting facilities. Living closer to each other, the same programme could be spread over weekday evenings.

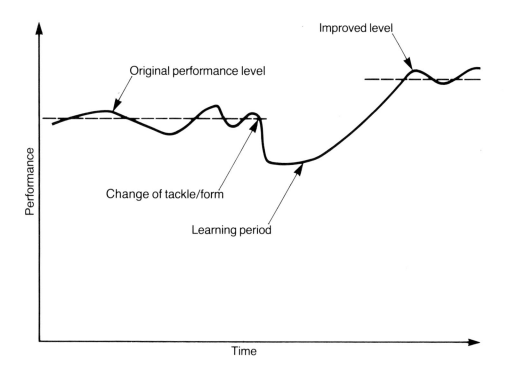

Effect of changes

When coach and archer first get together they will be tempted to rush into analysis, diagnosis and training programme. Avoid it; there is plenty of time, even with a major contest not far off. The archer must get used to shooting in the presence of the coach, he must accept that the coach is not there to criticise but to help – even though he has already paid lip service to the idea. At the same time the coach has to discover all he can about the archer from observation, direct discussion, gentle and tactful questioning and also socially where archery is not directly involved.

Then, if remedial training is needed as in dealing with variable shooting patterns or in relieving tensions, the archer will be more ready to accept advice and instruction.

While the coach is observing the archer he is assessing the needs of that archer and deciding priorities in dealing with the outward and visible aspects of the archer's shooting. He has to distinguish between symptoms and causes and he has to find out why the archer does things in a particular way – for example, supporting the bow preparatory to drawing and shooting may have developed as the most comfortable means of coping with the physical weight of added stabilisers.

A variable and often weak release of the string may originate in unbalanced posture, which in turn would inhibit full and effective use of back and shoulders in drawing the bow and taking the shot through aim and release into the follow through.

More of a problem is the case where the archer seems to do everything that he should but where the results at the target do not match the making of the shot. Sometimes this could be due to a lack of real motivation, sometimes to a lack of visual co-ordination, sometimes to the body not being pointed towards the target centre with consequent attempts at fine adjustment under load and sometimes to an unsuitable draw weight. Only a coach working with the archer can pinpoint the source of the trouble, and that not immediately. This is not an area where miracles occur.

Practice in practice

What is practice? The dictionary offers little help: 'repeated exercise in an art, handicraft, etc'. It is better to ask why an archer finds it necessary to practise. Four clear reasons are immediately apparent and doubtless readers will think of others:

a) so that muscular co-ordination is maintained
b) so that the necessary staying power for competition is developed
c) so that modifications in the form suggested by the coach can be adopted and consolidated
d) so that conscious effort to establish a pattern in the archer's shooting form becomes an unconsciously instinctive sequence of actions.

For an archer practice must be purposeful. Merely to go to the club to shoot because everybody else will be there and shooting is no good reason. It will be a nice social occasion and most enjoyable but it will not be practice in the true sense. However there is no reason why the archer should not take advantage of the social occasion and still put in purposeful practice. He may be shooting in a new batch of strings he has just made, he may be checking sight calibration before a tournament, he may be checking on shooting form (with his coach as observer) to make sure that all is well or he may be developing concentration on the shooting line – if he can close his ears to the badinage of the other club members while he is shooting he has developed a valuable supporting skill.

How much practice does an archer need as a preliminary to an important tournament, or indeed at any other time? One might as well ask 'how long is a piece of string?' It is governed by individual needs and by the precise purpose of the practice. There is only one answer; just as long as necessary and not one shot more. The steady, persistently plodding individual will want to shoot more before he is satisfied while the mercurial type with rapid reactions may be satisfied with far fewer shots, but it will vary from occasion to occasion. There are no set rules. Correction; there is one golden rule — just because archer A has achieved success as an international competitor it does not mean that the amount of practice he puts in would suit any other archer, so this golden rule is never to copy the procedures of any other archer, but to just do what is necessary at the time. It is like examination revision — the candidate is conscious of his own strengths and weaknesses and attends to his own needs. He is not revising for anyone else. And this is the advice any good coach will give — archer, know thyself!

Does all coaching have to be on the shooting range? Only when matters of outward and visible shooting form are under consideration and the practical elements call for modification.

Many archery coaches have claimed that their most effective coaching achievements have been conceived and even brought to full term in a social, non-shooting environment — over a cup of coffee, a jug of beer, in cafe, bar or by the fireside.

Such coaching gives the archer the chance to ask questions, discuss objectives, outline personal circumstances and get to know the coach while at the same time — and without the distractions of shooting and of equipment — the coach is finding out more about the archer as a person than ever he would on the archery field.

CHAPTER NINE

More about equipment

It is often said that successful shooting is almost entirely a function of the person holding the bow and that of that function, about 90 per cent is mental input and only about 10 per cent is physical. Similarly the archer's function is about 90 per cent of the whole leaving only 10 per cent for equipment. This is why equipment – except for the beginner – has been glossed over until now.

Listening to discussions whenever archers gather together would seem to belie this, for much attention is focussed upon merits and demerits of makes and designs of a great variety of equipment used by archers. Perhaps this is because most archers are somewhat incoherent when it comes to talking about physical input and even more so when it comes to mental input into the act of shooting.

The truth is that equipment for archery can be purchased. The skills and control of the equipment can only be developed with patience and perseverance. It is an unfortunate human weakness that often archers delude themselves into thinking that the purchase of increasingly costly bows, arrows and accessories can serve as a substitute for time and effort.

In an everchanging world the quoting of current prices and mention of specific makes and models of equipment items can only mislead. A sound rule of thumb is to take as a target figure something that is about 40–50 per cent of the top of the range prices. In general there will be a fairly wide choice of items at around the target figure that will give good service and have an inbuilt standard of accuracy more precise than can be provided by the archer who uses them. Another factor is that of rates of exchange between one currency and another. Again, a rough rule of thumb is that imported equipment is likely to be about 50 per cent more costly than the equivalent native product.

Any beginner who has mastered the skills of archery sufficiently to graduate to his first competition bow will in due time want to go further. He will want a bow that enables him to compete as accurately and as successfully as his level of skill will allow at the maximum target archery distances or that will give him an acceptably low trajectory in field archery.

This generally means an increase in the draw weight of the bow compared with that he has previously used. Such an increase best can be achieved by fitting stiffer limbs of the same length to the same handle. Where the archer has begun his competitive career with a one-piece bow his choice, as he progresses, will be from among a wide variety of take-down bows. One-piece bows are rare today in the dealers' catalogues.

Compound bows

Compound bows (those that offer a mechanical advantage through the use of pulleys or cams) are now widely advertised, though their presence on the archery field is far less common than would be supposed from the advertising.

Because of the mechanical advantage the bows offer to their users, archers with compound bows must compete in a class separate from that for recurve bows, again with all the subdivisions of male and female, senior and junior, member and visitor, apart from further subdivisions depending substantially on whether the string is shot off the fingers or from a release aid. This is an added complication for tournament organisers who might not encourage competitors to use compound bows, though in the United Kingdom they cannot exclude them from tournaments.

FITA currently makes no provision for compound bows in major international competitions. There is support for continuing to limit these competitions to recurve bows from those national bodies that would have to finance entry fees, travel and accommodation for two teams instead of one as at present. This problem already exists to some extent in field archery where there are two classes in major international competitions, free style and bare bow.

However, for those whose strength in arms, back or shoulders is impaired through age, illness or accident, the compound bow allows the archer to continue to enjoy the pleasures of shooting in the bow. Through the mechanical advantage such bows give, the draw weight the archer has to contend with at full draw is about half that of the bow's peak weight – in other words a compound bow with a peak weight of 50lb will feel at full draw very much like a recurve of 25lb draw weight.

Purists will say that the compound bow is inelegant in appearance and dislike it for that reason. This machinelike appearance is the price the archer has to pay if he needs that mechanical advantage. The image of the compound bow has been further tarnished by its use in certain widely distributed films, reflecting the trend in certain countries where bow hunting dominates and where the compound has swamped the recurve so that the latter is seldom seen except where the archers are looking to FITA and the Olympics.

It must be realised that the compound is here to stay. In the United

The compound bow used with release aid is ideal for wheelchair archers. Note how the bow-string is well clear of both chest and chair

Kingdom its numbers seem likely to increase, though not to the extent that it would dominate competitive archery. Enough are now in use to give the lie to old wives' tales that they cause extensive damage to the target bosses; early specimens were of hunting rather than target weights while, even with release aids, levels and peep sights, they are only as accurate as the archers who use them allow them to be.

Stabilisation

Up to a point it is easier to hold a comparatively heavy object steady than an extra light object. So it is with bows – the first steps in this direction lay in making the handle section heavier. Then followed the addition of weights external to the handle, first fixed directly to the bow and then extended from it on rods so that the centre of mass of the bow ended up at a point beyond the handle. All this served to slow down the movement of the bow in the hand and of the front arm that begins immediately the string is released.

The hold on the bow

This is crucial to any stabiliser array in use today. Contact between hand and handle must be just right so that the total pressure from the front arm via the hand is directly towards the target both before and immediately after the string has been let go. Although interchangeable 'grips' ('grip' is a manufacturers' term – no archer in his right mind will ever grip the handle) are made for many bows to allow variation of wrist position from high to low, they cannot be manufactured to suit every archer's hand. In the end the serious archer may have to tailor the handle to suit himself for the best results – sometimes by carving a bit off or, more commonly, by building up the handle with a resin-based filler.

The bow sling

An important companion to the handle of the right shape is the bow sling. With bow hand open and relaxed as it should be and without a sling nothing can stop the forward movement of the bow on the release and it will leave the hand and fall to the ground. The sling allows this forward movement to continue until the arrow has cleared the string and then stops it so that the bow remains in the hand. Several types are on the market but the cheapest, and at the same time the most popular with leading performers, is the corded

The compound bow in action at the 1987 UK Masters Tournament, Chorley, Lancashire

Harmony on the shooting line. Long bows, compound bows and recurve bows share the shooting line at the 1987 Berkshire County Championships

sling. This has a loop round the wrist with the loose end taken round the bow, usually between first and second finger of the bow hand, the hook at the end taken back and secured to the loop round the wrist. It is fully adjustable to suit the individual and holds the bow higher on the handle than most other types, thus reducing acrobatic movement of the bow.

Which stabiliser?
Back to stabilisers now – with handle modified to suit the archer, his hand is relaxed and the sling is adjusted correctly. The next question is what kind of stabilisation should be fitted. Perhaps it should be rephrased as 'do I need any stabilisers?'

Stabilisation is very much an individual matter; there are a great many combinations of mountings, weights and rod lengths. It is possible to spend as much, if not more, on stabilisers than on the bow itself. Is this wise? So this is where the archer must first get his shooting form together (for no stabiliser system will make up for variable shooting technique) and then allow time for some trials.

One danger exists for young people. They are still growing and developing both their bone structure and their muscles, a process that sometimes continues almost into the early twenties. Adding weights to the bow puts an undesirable load on young muscles while causing rapid fatigue and a possible breakdown in technique. The only way round this is a 'softly, softly' approach, keeping the load to a minimum and intensifying training if this is possible and compatible with studies.

The long rod

Knowing how he groups his arrows in the unstabilised mode, the archer can begin his trials. The single long rod is a key element in most systems and the one with fewest complications. This is attached just below the handle and points towards the target. The centre of mass of the bow is taken forward of the handle and slightly below it. On the release it will cause the bow to tilt forward in the hand whereas the unstabilised bow will remain roughly upright. The essence of the long rod is that in use it is rigidly screwed into the handle section of the bow. It consists of a light tapered rod in aluminium or carbon fibre about 25 to 30in long (625 to 780mm) with a weight at the end. The very length of the rod serves to damp down any oscillation due to the effect of movement on this weight.

Since the bow tilts forward following the loose, a lot of thought has gone into devising additional systems of attached weights to reduce both the amount and the rate of movement of the bow. The same amount of thought does not go into the archer's choice of additional weights and their location – he sees what other archers use and decides to have some of the same!

Engineers maintain that the ideal combination of stabilising weights would result in the centre of mass of the stabilised bow coinciding with the centre of pressure of the bow hand on the handle. Observation of the systems favoured by leading performers suggests that the centre of mass is slightly below and forward of the centre of pressure.

Supplementing the long rod

One system adopted by more slightly built archers has the long rod already mentioned together with weights on shorter rods (commonly called twins) attached to the upper and lower extremities of the handle section and pointing forward roughly towards the target. Since these rods are shorter they can transmit vibrations to the handle so they are interfaced by flexible couplings (for which someone has dreamed up the name 'torque flight compensator' – 'TFC' for short). These couplings or dampers are adjustable from an almost rigid state to a quite floppy extreme. Such a system gives an all up weight of the stabilised bow of about 4lb (1.8kg).

Another system commonly used by more robust archers retains the long rod and the upper of the two rods of the previous system. An additional mounting, known as a vee-bar, is inserted where the long rod is usually attached. This takes the long rod plus two short rods with TFCs and weights attached. These short rods are usually mounted to point downwards and backwards (in V-shape) at about 45° to the centre line of the bow. The bow plus such a system is likely to have an all up weight of about 5lb (2.3kg), so an archer with a bow thus equipped will at a major tournament have lifted at least 750lb (345kg) in the course of shooting a single round.

This is the place to make the point that the more attachments the archer fits to his bow the longer it will take to assemble and check before shooting and the longer it will take to pack away afterwards. The more nuts, screws and bolts there are, the more items there are to work loose unbeknown to the archer. His routine will not now be just one of shooting but will also include a routine of checking every single fastening that holds his tackle together.

The good and competent archer will have built up his stabiliser system step by step, testing it thoroughly at each stage, at the same time making sure that his form is up to a standard he can honestly accept. This takes time and application − it cannot be rushed.

The combinations of stabilisers described above are only two of many. Who knows when another fashion for something different may take over? Today this is less likely − the stabilisation described has been around for more than a decade.

Competition bow sights
It is possible to buy bow sights that cost more than many bows. The bulk of this expense seems to be in the limited production of finely machined components and in the use of carbon fibre for some of them so as to reduce the overall weight. Is such expenditure justified?

The more costly sights all have adjustable forward extensions, some as much as 15in (38cm) long, detachable from their mountings for safe transit leaving the mount permanently attached to the bow. All have side mounts for which most bows today have the handle section bushed ready to receive them.

The only snag with such sights, apart from their cost, is that they are vulnerable to damage. They also attract a lot of fiddling by their users − partly through checking that the locking devices have not worked loose, partly an almost reflex action of adjustment after every shot regardless of whether it is necessary. Since the mounting is off centre, stabilisation can also be affected.

A recent trend suggests that some successful performers are bringing their sights back from the extreme end of the extension to a point roughly one third of the extension's length away from the bow. It will be interesting to see whether this trend continues − those who initiated it seem happy.

For the sight itself there is a wide choice beginning with the simple ring and pin with which most archers start. From the psychological point of view this is by no means the best. The bead on the end of the pin partially obsures the centre of the mark at which the archer aims, so he will try to look round the bead to see it while at the same time trying to keep the bead steady on the mark. This is contradictory and there has to be a solution.

112

In fact there are two solutions – one is the aperture. Some manufacturers offer a selection of apertures of varying diameters that can easily be fitted into the basic ring, thus allowing the archer to change apertures according to the quality of the light or the distance at which he is shooting. The aperture allows the archer to see the whole target, or as much of it as he wants, without having to peer round the bead. Further, the combination of circular aperture and circular target initiates a certain self-centring action.

The other choice is the interrupted cross – a cross where the intersection of the horizontal and vertical members has been cut back to stumps projecting from the surrounding ring. Again, the projection of these stumps encourages a self-centring effect with positive indication of vertical and lateral alignment.

It is physically impossible for an archer to hold his bow absolutely rock steady so that the sight does not move from its alignment with the target centre although many archers are unwise enough to try. Far better that he should allow the sight to 'float' in the general area of the mark. If his body is correctly aligned and if he has full control of the load applied to the bow then the release will come as the sight seems to gently float towards the target centre. If the bow sight has to be forced onto the line of sight, then something is very wrong with the way the shot has been put together.

Remember that the prime function of any bow sight is to enable the archer to achieve a constant amount of elevation with every shot that he makes. The possible lateral movement of the sight represents a very fine traversing adjustment. Even simple commercial bow sights will meet these requirements.

Arrows

An important complement to the bow is a good set of arrows. Once more the guiding principle is to obtain arrows of local manufacture in preference to those imported, if this is at all possible. The same guidelines on prices set out for bows will apply here. There are several different suppliers of good medium priced arrows in tubing drawn from 7075 alloy. Today the makers of these arrows all supply 'bullet' or ogival points, a significant improvement upon the conical points which were all that manufacturers would supply a few years ago.

The qualities of an arrow for competition purposes are that it should be matched to bow and archer for length, weight, balance, diameter and stiffness. Most archery dealers include in their catalogues tables of suitable dimensions in relation to arrow length and draw weight of bow. Where the charts or tables do not give tube sizes for 7075 alloy shafts the XX75 indication will be a very near equivalent. Such charts are a good starting point for selecting arrows, though many archers today will find that they can use slightly stiffer shafts than indicated by these charts.

113

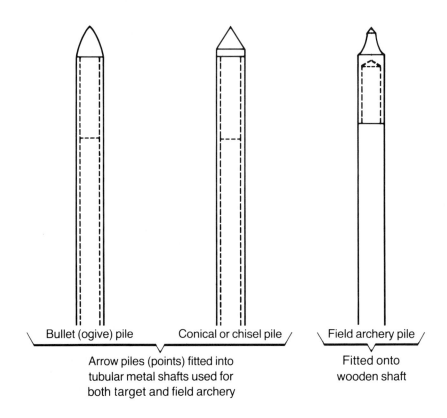

Bullet (ogive) pile | Conical or chisel pile | Field archery pile

Arrow piles (points) fitted into tubular metal shafts used for both target and field archery

Fitted onto wooden shaft

Arrow points

Contrary to what most archers seem to believe, speed of arrow flight is probably the least important factor in determining the set up of the bow and the choice of arrows to go with it. Equipment forgiving of very small variations in shooting form, that allows simple tuning and gives tight formation of groups, is much more important. Similarly, absolute precision in specification for a set of arrows is not as significant as some would insist. There are tolerances; one authority says of straightness that a deviation of 0.004in (0.1mm) per ft (30cm) has no measurable effect on the grouping of the arrows, while an overall difference in a set of arrows of something like 1–1.5 per cent in weight between lightest and heaviest will not be noticed in practical application.

Fletching arrows for use in serious competition calls for care and attention. The function of the vanes is to stabilise the arrow during the flexing that occurs at the beginning of its flight and that gives it directional stability as it continues towards the target. The vanes give consistent and stable flight when they are set on the shaft so that it spins around its longitudinal axis. In most common use are flat plastics vanes, offset on the shaft by about 2° relative to its axis. Authorities are divided on whether there is any merit in rotating the shaft clockwise or anticlockwise in flight according to the handedness of the archer. In most instances it is probably of little significance. Although some archers swear by vanes of different sizes or of distinctive profiles, the majority will benefit from steering a middle course, avoiding expensive eccentricities.

Cleanliness and accuracy are the watchwords when fletching arrows – the use of an oil-free solvent (with all the care that use of solvents demands) to clean both shaft and the base of the vane is important to ensure a lasting bond between vane and shaft, while a good quality adhesive formulated specially for the purpose justifies the greater cost than for household adhesives. The competent archer who attends to his own fletching knows very well that he has only himself to blame if things are not done as well as they should be.

Bowstrings

These have been mentioned before in Chapters 3 and 7. The tried and tested materials that archers are familiar with are Dacron (in two versions: B50 and B66) and kevlar. Dacron B66 is a newer material, heralded as a compromise between B50 and kevlar being claimed to be less stretchy and elastic than B50 while having the same property of long life. The same manufacturer/distributor has lately introduced 'Fast Flight', which is claimed to have the life of five times that of kevlar while sharing the same non-stretch characteristic.

For a given quantity the cost of the materials is roughly in the ratio:

$$B50-1: B66-1\frac{1}{2}: kevlar-2\frac{1}{2}: Fast Flight-3\frac{1}{2}$$

The differential will be less for bought strings because there is little difference between materials in the time taken to make a complete string.

The archer who makes his own strings can effect considerable savings compared with buying similar ready made strings, and – as with the arrows he has fletched himself – he will have only himself to blame if the strings he has made turn out to be variable in quality.

Revolutionary designs and materials

From time to time revolutionary designs of bows, arrows and accessories are introduced and similarly new materials, first used in space or military hardware, are applied to the making of archery equipment.

Occasionally the new ideas have really taken off and are now fully accepted in archery – compound bows for example. Other ideas have foundered because of structural weaknesses, because they were ahead of their time, or because they were aesthetically unpleasing. Yet others have been priced so high that the archery public totally rejected them.

Likewise with materials – when they first appear they seem to be the ideal solution in terms of strength or of lightness. However new materials run into production problems and the cost of items that incorporate new materials remains high. In certain uses the qualities representing a positive gain in lightness or strength are offset by hidden snags – the user has to consider whether or not the inbuilt defects outweight the undoubted merits. Kevlar as a bowstring material is typical – for the disciplined and highly competitive archer its unvarying qualities more than compensate for the short life and additional cost but for the vast majority of archers any real gain is doubtful.

There are always those who must have the very latest of everything regardless of whether it suits them – their opinions need to be treated with some caution. The serious competitor will talk to his coach and to his peers to see whether he might gain from experimenting with anything new, always having in mind that new items might not have been seen and approved by the governing bodies in the sport. In time he will decide for himself on the item's qualities and adopt or discard accordingly.

Miscellaneous items

Numerous accessories come under this heading but cannot be called minor because today they are in widespread use and because to many archers they are important aids to successful shooting. Their mention here is by no means in order of merit – in this context all have equal weight.

The platform tab

When the archer has a centre of the chin reference point he can control eye to nock distance and keep it constant through contact between first finger and chin. It is skin to skin contact and a well drilled archer will have little difficulty here. However if it becomes clear that an archer will make more effective shots with a side of face reference point there comes a time when the string is moved so far away from the centre that forefinger contact is no longer a positive aid to constant eye to nock distance and substantial vertical error is possible. Here the platform tab can help. Attached to the tab is a solid platform extended sufficiently so that there is contact between platform and the underside of the jaw giving a firm reference in the vertical plane.

Many tabs on the market have a so-called anti-pinch device attached, a block that fits between first and second fingers. Its use prevents the extreme pressure of fingers on the arrow stemming from incorrect location of the fingers on the string preparatory to making the shot, though the fingers still bear down hard on the block. Note that many leading performers do not use an anti-pinch device because their attention to detail in preparing and making the shot renders it unnecessary.

Draw checks

As its name implies a draw check is an attachment that tells an archer when his arrow is fully drawn. There are two types, visual and audible. The former, employing either mirror or a pop-up device, are rarely seen. It is the audible device, called a clicker for obvious reasons, that is widely used today.

There is still considerable debate as to its proper use. Certainly when correctly used it has great potential for improving the pattern of an archer's shooting and all that goes with it. However its use is not obligatory and archers should be wary of using it until their shooting technique is both efficient and consistent.

It is easy to attach a clicker to a bow. What is not so easy is to attach it in the right place. The archer needs an assistant to watch him shoot and he must shoot sufficient arrows *at a tournament pace* so that he is thoroughly settled into his normal shooting form. This may be wearisome for the assistant, but by the end of two to three dozen arrows the assistant will have a very clear picture of where the arrow point ends up immediately before the release and the extent of any variations and he can mark the bow accordingly. It is sensible to mark graduations on masking tape and fix it to the bow in line with the arrow to identify where the arrow point is located.

Such a mark indicates only the location of the arrow point. The placing of the clicker has yet to be decided. Its position must allow for some minute variations in the archer's form – after all the archer is only human – but it must steer between the extremes of being so difficult for the archer to take the arrow through the clicker smoothly so that it is violently disturbed when the shot is made, and of being so easy that the shot is made before the archer is truly ready for it. A good starting point has the edge of the clicker nearest to the archer (the working edge) touching the pile of the arrow about half way between the very point and the place where it attains maximum diameter. Typically the length of a bullet pile might be $\frac{5}{16}$in (8mm) so the working edge of the clicker would contact this pile about $\frac{5}{32}$in (4mm) from the point.

The archer sets up his shot – in his field of view the sight floats around the centre of the target and instinct tells him that all is well – but the arrow is still keeping the clicker away from the bow. If the archer's mind is properly tuned he will have a secondary image of what happens after the loose. He knows that freedom from the restraint of the drawn bow will take his back elbow rearwards quite a way and move that back elbow round behind his head. All he has to do is to initiate that rearward movement at the instant he senses that the shot is complete apart from the actual release. As set out in Chapter 4, the loose is something that occurs between the development of the hold and the rounding off of the follow through.

The archer will not know when the clicker will click – the sound will be something of a surprise to him when it happens even though it is expected –

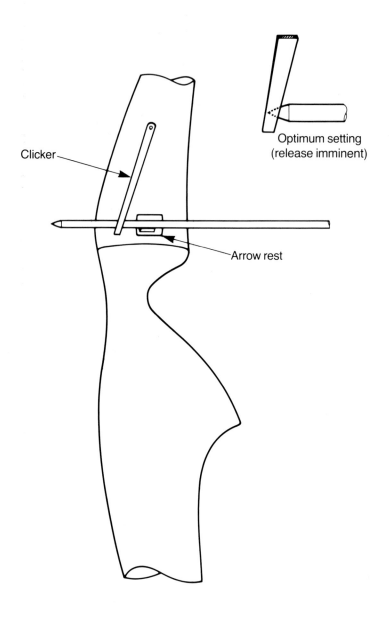

Clicker

Optimum setting
(release imminent)

Arrow rest

The clicker: location and use

the shot is balanced on a knife edge at that instant just waiting for something to make it fall, like the surprise of the click. Quoting from Herrigel's book *Zen in the Art of Archery*:

> It is all so simple. You can learn from an ordinary bamboo leaf what ought to happen. It bends lower and lower under the weight of snow. Suddenly the snow slips to the ground without the leaf having stirred. Stay like that at the point of highest tension until the shot falls from you. So, indeed it is: when the tension is fulfilled, the shot *must* fall, it must fall from the archer like snow from a bamboo leaf, before he even thinks it.

Because the position of the clicker has been determined by the archer's way of shooting it serves another very useful purpose. If the archer frequently experiences difficulty in moving the arrow back past the clicker or finds that the arrow has come through the clicker sooner than expected, this should tell him that there has been a change in his way of shooting. The clicker was set up to work with an established technique, which has for the moment broken down.

There is nothing wrong with the clicker or its positioning. Leave it alone! The solution to the immediate problem lies elsewhere – don't panic; that only makes matters worse – stay cool, calm and collected. Remember the good shots – after all the clicker is an inert strip of metal that harms no one – and just get on with reproducing those shots.

Pressure buttons
In the beginning the arrow rested on the archer's hand. Eventually it was discovered that the hand could move up and down the handle, thus giving unwanted scatter of hits up and down the target. A shelf attached to or part of the handle section of the bow reduced this error, but unless this shelf was very narrow the vanes made contact with it – not quite so important when natural feather was in universal use but critical when plastics took over. Thus was the separate arrow rest born, located above the shelf, which in the end became the lower limit of the cut-out for the sight window as bows were designed more and more to allow the arrow to lie on or close to the centre line of the bow.

The arrow once rested against the side of the bow and many nineteenth and twentieth century long bows had a mother of pearl insert or arrow plate at that point to resist wear and tear. As the cut-out of the recurve bow was extended beyond the centre line of the bow it became necessary to fit an adjustable arrow plate. In due time the spring loaded version was introduced, now known as a pressure button.

Today all but the cheapest bows are bushed so that a pressure button may be fitted should the archer so desire – and most do. The button has two modes of adjustment – straightforward movement in and out along the axis of the button and increasing or decreasing the spring tension that holds the button in place against the sideways forces exerted by the arrow as it is released. Once they have been set up to suit the archer, the adjustments can be locked against accidental movement and the whole button assembly can be removed from the bow without upsetting them.

Adjustments of pressure and position are made when first setting up the bow for shooting and then should need no further attention while the archer's shooting form and equipment remain unchanged.

Most arrow rests now available are designed with use of the pressure button in mind. Do not be confused by terminology. The pressure button has different names: compensator button, plunger button and Berger button (named after the archer who developed it). There may even be others but these are the most common.

The chest guard

Many archers are built in such a way that even when shooting correctly the string lays well into the chest and passes quite close to the shoulder. In such cases clothing can easily catch the bowstring and take the shot away from the main group. A chest guard presents a smooth surface to the string with sufficient rigidity so that it will not fold and deflect the string, while at the same time keeping the clothing under control.

Bracing height gauge

With a take-down bow the string has to be removed from the bow whenever it is dismantled after shooting and replaced after the bow has been put together for shooting. The string has been given a certain number of turns so that the twists hold it together and enable the string to be set at a constant bracing height. Repeated removal and replacement can alter this if the archer is careless and the bracing height gauge becomes a useful tool to check that all is well before and during shooting, especially if the string is new and being used for the first time. The best of such gauges also have scales that help to determine and check the location of the nocking point on the string relative to the perpendicular from arrow rest to bowstring.

Arrow puller

Target bosses today are much firmer than they were and grip the arrows more tightly. This grip is even tighter when the boss is wet, while a wet arrow is more difficult to hold firmly. Even a dry arrow is not easy to grip with the hand on account of its small diameter.

An arrow puller is a device held in the hand and clasped around the shaft under hand pressure. Its firm hold of the shaft together with its large-diameter ridged exterior enables the archer to withdraw the arrows without

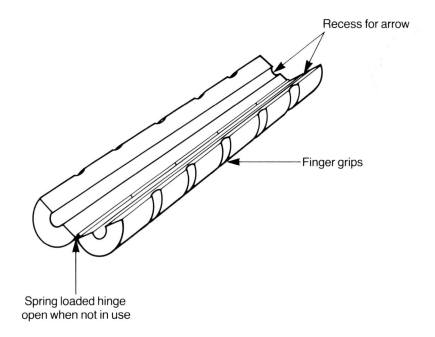

Recess for arrow

Finger grips

Spring loaded hinge
open when not in use

Arrow puller

difficulty from the toughest of targets. It is a useful item to carry in the tackle box.

Thread sizes – a warning
With stabilisers, pressure buttons and other attachments to bows it is important to note the thread sizes of the bushes fitted to take these attachments. There is no international standard for thread sizes though some uniformity does exist. ⁵⁄₁₆in bushes for long rod stabilisers and for pressure buttons seem to be standard on most makes though one perversely uses 8mm for the long rod. For twin stabilisers and reverse weights some bows are bushed with ⁵⁄₁₆in threads, others with ¼in threads and again one make uses 6mm.

The message is that the archer should be alert and make sure that any attachment he buys will fit his bow – the same caution applies whenever he changes his bow – namely that he can carry over his attachments from one bow to the next.

CHAPTER TEN

Tuning that bow

First principles

Anyone writing about bow tuning today will be taking the work of others and rearranging it in a pattern best suited to the intended readership. There are tried and tested routines that now feature even in dealers' catalogues.

There is a bit of a chicken and egg situation here. To tune tackle effectively requires that the archer has a certain consistency of performance. On the other hand, if the archer is suspicious of untuned equipment he is unlikely to realise his true potential in shooting. It has been said that a third class archer will only achieve third class tuning. Nonetheless certain basic items can be likened to the running in of a new car or the working up of a newly commissioned ship and its crew.

In taking possession of a bow, an archer will want the best possible performance from it compatible with his way of shooting. What does he mean by performance? Is it perfect arrow flight, a smooth feel to the way the bow shoots, the tightest possible groups at the target or the highest possible scores?

When people first started talking about tuning a bow they created an air of mystery around the process. And yet archers have always talked about setting the nocking point in the correct position, obtaining the optimum bracing height and the matching of their arrows to the bow; so what was new in the concept of tuning?

Preparation for tuning

It is assumed that the arrows have been selected using the selection charts so that they should match the bow and leave it cleanly. Whether they do so in practice will remain to be seen as the tuning process develops.

One of the first things an archer needs to find out is how the new bow behaves as it is first put together after purchase. The initial setting up has to be systematic. Stage one is to fit the string so that the bracing height is slightly on the high side of the midpoint of the recommended range (slightly higher than 10in [25.4cm] if the range is from 9½ [24cm] to 10½in [27cm]). There may be an initial settling down, particularly with a new and unused string.

A temporary nocking point is fitted using adhesive tape or dental floss so that it is about ³⁄₁₆–¼in (4–6mm) above the perpendicular from arrow rest to string. This is enough to get on with if no pressure button is fitted. Then the archer can start getting used to the bow before attempting to make any changes in either variable.

If a button is fitted, he has two additional variables to contend with. Spring pressure inside the button is adjusted so that when the button is pressed vertically downwards onto the scale pan of some household scales they give a reading of about 20oz (570gm). The pressure adjustment is then locked.

The button must be fitted into place on the bow before lateral adjustment can be made. This adjustment is made visually; an arrow is nocked and the archer lines up the string with the centre line of the bow. The button is screwed out until the axis of the arrow is seen to coincide with the string alignment, and then screwed out farther so that the apparent offset of the arrow at its point from the centre line is within the range ⅛–¼in (3–6mm). This lateral adjustment is then locked against further movement.

In this way the bow is set up so that there is a reasonable chance that all will be well when it is first used, the arrows leaving the bow cleanly.

The archer has been using other bows before taking over this new one, so it is worth looking at some of the peripherals in this running-in process. In the excitement of shooting with a new bow they could be overlooked – hold on the handle, wear and tear of the tab, the fit of the arrow nocks on the nocking point of the new string, string contact with the body. The different feel of a new bow can cause an archer to make minor and unsuspected adjustments of body position in relation to the drawn bow. At this stage the archer can never take things for granted.

Tuning – bare shaft planing test (or comparative method)

On discharge, the arrow will display characteristic movements in the vertical plane, known to some as 'porpoising', and in the horizontal plane, often called 'fishtailing'. Tuning greatly reduces such tendencies if not completely eliminating them.

Tuning procedures must be followed with care. The archer should shoot every arrow as if taking part in a tournament. Sight setting should be constant – the range will be short and the emphasis will be on where the arrows strike relative to each other.

The bracing height

The archer is seeking that bracing height which gives the minimum noise when the shot is delivered and which, at the same time, causes the least shock or vibration in the hand. He cannot really get on with further tuning until this is established.

A bracing height that is slightly greater than the middle of the manufacturer's recommended range generally allows a smoother feel to the way the bow shoots. Within limits the bracing height can be varied by twisting or untwisting the string – but some residual twist should always be left while the performance will certainly be affected if the string is twisted excessively. Some archers will make extra strings, each about ½in (1.2cm) longer or shorter than the one before to extend the range of adjustment.

The nocking point

The next priority is a more precise location for the nocking point. The initial setting mentioned above ensures that the archer starts off in the right direction. Now he has to work for improvement. The bare shaft planing method requires the archer to work with three fletched arrows and three shafts with exactly the same specification, but without fletchings. His sight setting will be constant – so also should be the aiming mark on the target. Also he must shoot the arrows a sufficient number of times in each part of the test to be sure that chance effects are eliminated. The distance best suited to these tests is about 15yd (14m).

If the nocking point has been set correctly in the first place, it is a bonus for the archer and both bare and fletched shafts will hit the target at the same height. If the bare shafts strike below the fletched ones, then the nocking point is too high and must be lowered – and vice versa. It may call for several trials before the archer can be sure he has got it right.

The pressure button

With nocking point established, the archer can look at lateral deviation in the same way. Where unfletched arrows strike left of the fletched arrows the shaft is too stiff, while bare shafts striking to the right indicate that the shaft is too flexible (this in terms of the right-handed archer). The left-handed archer must reverse his thinking in this respect. Without a pressure button the only solution is to try a different set of arrows, but this is less likely when a button is used.

There are two possible adjustments for the button, lateral location and spring pressure. The former is easier because the button does not have to be removed from the bow. Where the bare shafts strike to the right of the fletched shafts the button is moved to the left to increase the amount of offset, while the offset is reduced if the bare shafts strike to the left.

Often this may be sufficient but if not then the spring pressure is the last resort. Pressure is reduced if the bare shafts still strike to the left of the fletched arrows or increased if they still strike to the right.

Most archers find this method of setting up the equipment is adequate for their needs. Even so, it pays to keep a log of exactly what they have done, when and in what sequence.

Every time they make a change in equipment or in shooting form, they will need to run a quick check on tuning using this comparative method with bare shafts and fletched shafts. Thus they can see whether the changes they have made have upset their tuning and can do something about it if need be.

Tuning and fatigue

Unless the archer is superbly fit and thoroughly conditioned to much tournament shooting, fatigue may make itself felt towards the end of the day. It is wise, having established optimum settings for nocking point and pressure button, to make allowance for this.

Such allowances will vary from archer to archer but more recent recommendations suggest that it helps to have the nocking point slightly higher than the ideal established by the tests and to have the button slightly farther away from the bow or to increase the pressure by a small amount. With this the bare shafts would be expected to strike slightly lower and slightly to the left (for a right-handed archer) compared with the fletched arrows.

The walk-back method – an alternative approach to tuning

The bare shaft method does not satisfy everybody – many archers prefer an alternative approach. Again, no progress can be made until the position of the nocking point is established.

The archer first shoots several fletched arrows at the same mark at a distance of about 10yd/m and then one unfletched arrow of the same specification. If this arrow hits higher than the fletched shafts, then the nocking point must be raised, but if the impact is lower than the group then the nocking point must be lowered.

At the same time there are indications of the degree of stiffness of the arrows. The bare shaft landing left of the group (for a right-handed archer as are all references that follow) will indicate too stiff an arrow, while the bare shaft to the right points to an arrow that is not stiff enough. Now comes the work to compensate for this mismatch.

First set the sight for 20yd (18m) then, aiming at a mark near the top of the target shoot one (or two) fletched arrows at each of several distances from 10 up to 30 or 35yd (or metres) without any adjustment of the sight. If everything is as it should be, the arrows shot at each distance will form a pattern of hits in a vertical line from top to bottom of the target.

If the pattern first curves to the left and then back to the centre, the button should be moved to the right, but to the left if the pattern first curves to the right and then back to the centre.

Diagonal but straight line patterns indicate a need to adjust spring pressure; from top left to bottom right requiring an increase, while the

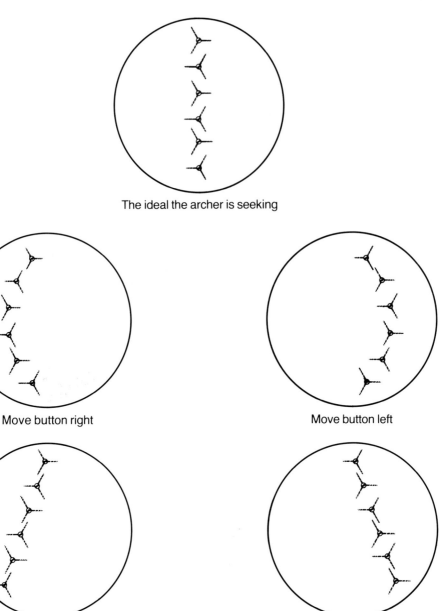

The ideal the archer is seeking

Move button right

Move button left

Reduce spring tension

Increase spring tension

The walk-back method of bow tuning: arrow patterns

opposite pattern from top right to bottom left calls for a reduction.

If no button is fitted, then possible alternatives could include an increased bracing height, fitting heavier piles to the arrows or the use of longer arrows to compensate for arrows that are too stiff and vice versa for arrows that are not stiff enough.

It is even possible to tune simple fibreglass bows using this method.

Experimentation

Most archers have little time for experiments to study the effects of particular changes in equipment or in shooting form. Of those that have the time, some may justifiably fear that, having made a change, they would be unable to return exactly to the original state.

Here keeping a log demonstrates its usefulness. The archer should concentrate on the equipment side and leave his shooting technique unchanged until he can work on it with his coach. All equipment details are matters of record, be they makers' specifications or weights, pressures or linear dimensions. It boils down to a simple 'before and after' study where the effect can also be recorded.

But remember the essential rule for 'before and after' studies; alter one factor at a time only and always leave a way open for a return to the original set-up.

Such experimentation is usually conducted at the intermediate outdoor distances and it demands that the archer is fully capable of shooting his arrows in recognisable groups at those distances before he attempts such an exercise.

CHAPTER ELEVEN

Field and Indoor Archery

So far only target archery has been described but much in earlier chapters will apply also to other disciplines.

What is field archery? It derives from a simulation of hunting where bow hunters wished to develop their skills before hunting expeditions or to maintain them during the close season.

Instead of shooting from a common shooting line towards a line of targets on a level field as in target archery, field archery involves groups of archers following round a course from target to target just as golfers go from green to green. The course is laid out to create variety, shooting up and down slopes, in and out of shade, across valleys or water, and at varying distances with different sizes of target.

Today it has developed into a challenging branch of the sport with its own major championships both under the auspices of FITA and in other associations independent of the recognised national and international governing bodies. The common bond is a love of archery – the differences are those of detail with the parties involved sadly being unwilling to compromise in the interests of unity.

The FITA field competitions may be more formal in some respects than those of the other bodies because, in bringing together many nations each with its own traditions and conventions, there is no place for a casual approach. For team selection or for the establishment of national and international records there must be comparability between one event and another. Nevertheless the essentials are preserved and field archery under FITA rules has a very large following.

The only thing that prevents this discipline from outstripping the numerically stronger target archery in the United Kingdom and most of Europe is the difficulty of setting up dedicated field courses and protecting them from the attentions of vandals, property developers and officialdom.

To incorporate the necessary variety calls for a large site (at least 12 acres or 5 hectares for 28 targets), not easy to find in densely populated areas where almost every square yard is farmed intensively, built upon or dedicated as public open space. Co-operative landowners, public or private, prepared to

*Roy Mundon, a notable British bare-bow field archer. Note that the bow is completely bare of sight and stabilisers and also the numbering of the arrows. The nock of the arrow is close to and immediately below the aiming eye (*The British Archer*)*

allow field archers access to their property are worth their weight in gold.

Techniques and equipment

Today FITA recognises two recurve bow classes, bare bow and free style. Free style archers use exactly the same equipment as in target archery except that aids for estimating distances and memoranda that assist in improving scores are not permitted and, when shooting unmarked distances, no field glasses or other visual aids are allowed. The serving on the bowstring must not end within the archer's field of vision at full draw. The free style archer retains the same shooting technique as in target competition.

The bare bow archer retains much that was traditional in bygone archery. Additional to the prohibitions applying to the free style archer, sights and draw check indicators are not permitted. The bow must be free from protrusions, marks, blemishes or laminations that could be of use in aiming. Trademarks are not permitted on the inside of the upper limb. TFCs are only allowed if they are an integral part of the bow and cannot be removed without causing damage, but they must not be fitted with stabilisers or added weights.

Arrow rests, arrow plates and pressure buttons are allowed and may be adjustable.

Experts have for many years maintained that free style shooting is the most effective foundation for ultimate development as a bare bow shooter. This trains the archer in pointing his body at the target and in obtaining the best load transfer from arms to back and shoulders so that the archer has adequate 'back tension' for making the shot. He will have effective control of body and bow and can recognise the sensations of being in full control.

Now he can attend to the development of his bare bow form. As a free style archer he has learned to adapt to the terrain, maintaining his shoulder line whether shooting downhill or uphill, and rotating at the hips so that wherever the feet are placed for stability his shot is properly pointed at the target.

It makes sense at this stage to use longer arrows; the change in technique can lead to a greater draw length than used in free style.

As was stressed earlier with target archery form, the aiming eye must be vertically above the nock of the arrow. Because bare bow techniques require the hand to be brought to the side of the face, the head must be inclined to the side to achieve this relationship – and of course the bow must remain vertical.

The archer trains to establish good posture so that he uses his body effectively, but keeps his head inclined and turned more fully towards the target than in free style when establishing his line of sight. The fingers are loaded on the string, the bow is presented to the target and the draw is completed with the hand making contact with the face. As in target archery the loose is the interface between completion of draw and follow through.

The result is that there will usually be greater clearance between string and body and that the back elbow will be brought more into line with the arrow, both beneficial to making a good shot.

Aiming techniques

The bare bow archer has the point of his arrow as his only aid to aiming. If he places its nock below, but very close to, his aiming eye the line of flight and line of sight will almost coincide at the shorter distances. But what about the longer distances? He must lift his bow to obtain the necessary elevation so the target will be hidden from view by hand and arm. Once this happens precision in aiming will be lost. To keep the target in view demands some other method.

One method is known as 'gapping' or 'gap shooting'; initially it assumes that the nock of the arrow is brought to the same point relative to the aiming eye for every shot and that as the range changes so the apparent vertical distance between target centre and arrow point also changes, decreasing as the range increases until the hand obscures the target. It is to the bare bow archer's advantage to use a bow that will give him the flattest possible trajectory at 60m, the maximum distance shot in FITA field archery. In this way it is still possible at this distance for there to be a small gap between arrow point and target.

Two other methods allow for the variation of distance from archer to target, face walking and string walking. In face walking the finger position on the string remains constant, usually three fingers just below the arrow, while the hand is brought to different positions against the face to increase the amount of elevation or depression. In string walking the fingers are placed in different positions on the string to obtain the necessary elevation or depression, moving the nock of the arrow up or down, while the hand is brought to the same position for every shot made.

The nature of the competition

The FITA Field Round consists of 112 arrows shot over 28 targets, four arrows at each target. Target face sizes range from 15cm to 60cm and distances from 6m to 60m, all distances being marked. There is a mixture of one-position targets where four arrows are shot from a single post and 'walk-up' shots where one arrow is shot from each of four posts in decreasing distance from the target.

Even with marked distances the archer can be deceived by gradient, crossfall, interplay of light and shade or by the apparent scale of objects close to the targets. Other sources of deception are shots across depressions, which may cause the target to seem closer, or across water where it may seem farther away.

Unmarked distances are the main feature of the FITA Hunters Round, which again requires a total of 112 arrows. Here the shots are all of the 'walk-up' sort with one arrow shot from each of four posts. Distances vary from 5 to 50m and target sizes from 15 to 60cm. Tournament organisers may mark distances but few do.

Archers must have their arrows numbered by plainly visible rings 3mm wide and 3mm apart so that on targets with multiple faces the arrows are shot in numerical order. Thus an arrow hitting the wrong face would be a miss and would not score.

There is a variety of rounds in field archery where the enjoyment of shooting is more evident, not that the FITA type competitions are by any means dull. In the United Kingdom under the auspices of the Grand National Archery Society there are four recognised rounds that provide

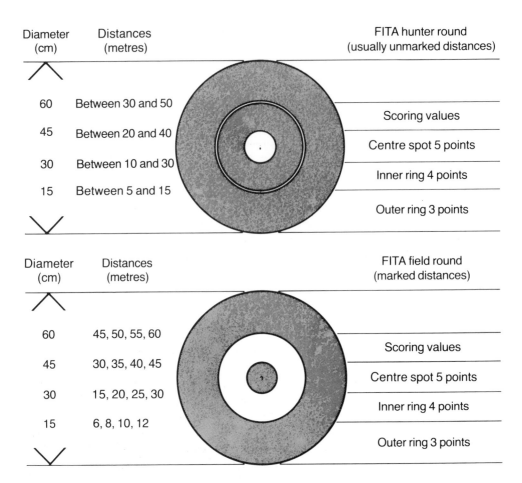

Diameter (cm)	Distances (metres)	FITA hunter round (usually unmarked distances)
60	Between 30 and 50	**Scoring values**
45	Between 20 and 40	Centre spot 5 points
30	Between 10 and 30	Inner ring 4 points
15	Between 5 and 15	Outer ring 3 points

Diameter (cm)	Distances (metres)	FITA field round (marked distances)
60	45, 50, 55, 60	**Scoring values**
45	30, 35, 40, 45	Centre spot 5 points
30	15, 20, 25, 30	Inner ring 4 points
15	6, 8, 10, 12	Outer ring 3 points

FITA field archery target faces

variety, enjoyment and a challenge to the skills of the archer. All four, foresters, four shot foresters, big game and national animal, use pictures of animals of various sizes as target faces, and are seen by some as more of a challenge than the black and white roundels of FITA rounds.

Provided that GNAS safety requirements are met and that rules of the competition are made known in advance to all competitors there is no bar to the shooting of many other traditional, overseas or local field archery rounds.

Safety
Because of the terrain over which a field archery round is shot, safety is of paramount importance. Great responsibility rests on the shoulders of those

whose task it is to set out the field course and on the judges who must check the safety of both course and practice area.

Since the groups of archers move from target to target until each group has shot at every one of the 28 targets of, say, a FITA Field Round it is important that no arrows are shot in any direction where archers or spectators would pass as they move from target to target. The provision of a 'safe path' enables officials and work parties to move quickly to any part of the course to replace faulty butts or where the archers call for a judge.

Uphill shots can be particularly hazardous; arrows shot above the target can become flight shots if there is no steeply rising ground beyond the target and no backstop netting.

Laying out an interesting and challenging course is a skill that cannot be set out in any textbook because every ground has different characteristics. Always remember that field archery is a test of an archer's shooting skills and not of his mountaineering ability; although if there are to be uphill and downhill shots some climbing is inevitable and interest would otherwise be lost.

Other weapons

Although major FITA contests cater only for recurve bows, domestic events have additional classes, even for the FITA rounds. In the United Kingdom the GNAS provides for other classes of bow.

There is the 'traditional' class which is the bare bow class with additional

Forester Round target in an open situation on level ground. Where most shots are on slopes and in shade this can take the archer by surprise

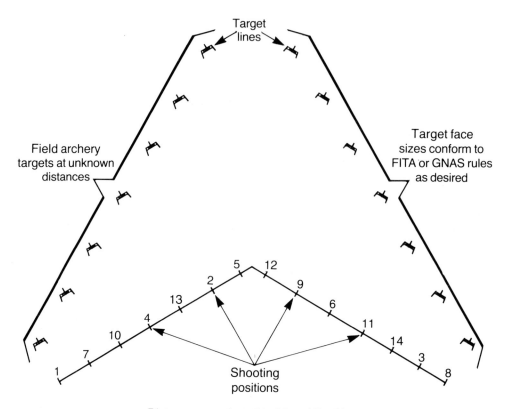

Field archery targets at unknown distances

Target face sizes conform to FITA or GNAS rules as desired

Distances vary from 6 to 60m while either
FITA or animal target faces can be used. Archers
move from target to target in numerical sequence
(with acknowledgements to Don Stamp et al)

An open field training layout for field archery

requirements that the arrows shall be made of wood, face and string walking are not permitted, pressure buttons are not allowed and the arrow rest must be fixed.

The compound bow appears in three different classes: 'unlimited', with no restrictions on the accessories used; 'limited', where the string must be drawn, held and released by the fingers and scopes are not allowed; and 'bow hunter', like the limited class, only with further curbs in that on bow or string no marking or attachment may appear that may be used as an aid to aiming and that only a single stabiliser, no more than 12in (30.5cm) long, is allowed.

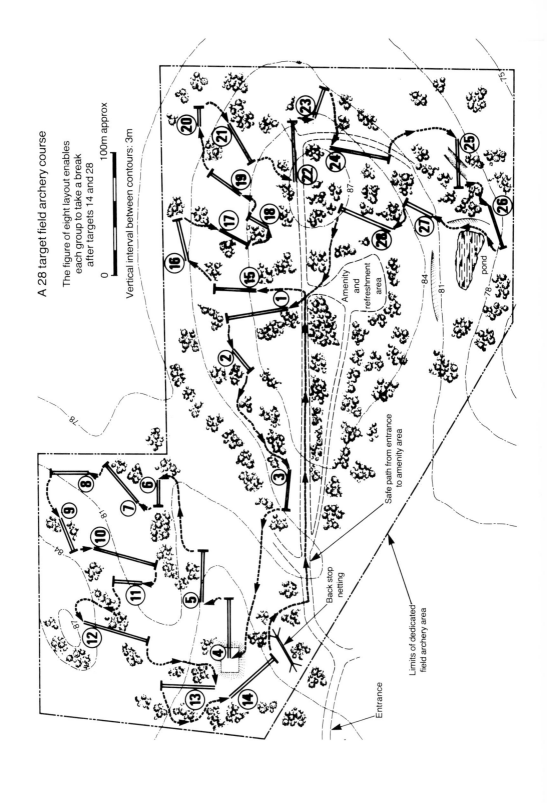

A 28 target field archery course

The figure of eight layout enables
each group to take a break
after targets 14 and 28

Vertical interval between contours: 3m

0   100m approx

Amenity
and
refreshment
area

Safe path from entrance
to amenity area

Back stop
netting

pond

Entrance

Limits of dedicated
field archery area

Crossbow archery is incorporated into the GNAS rules of shooting and in theory crossbows can be used in field archery, with the proviso that crossbowmen shall shoot on separate targets from other archers and shall not compete with them. Their use is uncommon in GNAS events.

Even without crossbows the multiplicity of classes of bow, subdivisions by age and sex and, for example, county and open cause enough problems for tournament organisers when it comes to preparing prize lists for an event.

Young people and field archery

The informality of field archery has its attractions when compared with target archery. The constant change of scene as the archers progress round the course, the inclusion of juniors with adults in each group instead of relegating them to the end of the shooting line in target archery and the concessions made for young people in the GNAS rules, all make field archery particularly attractive.

For many juniors the bare bow style of shooting seems natural and has proved to be more controllable for the younger juniors. It is not unknown for children of six or seven to be introduced to the bow through field archery, going round the course with their parents and shooting from privilege posts closer than usual to the targets.

Indoor archery

It is commonly thought that indoor archery is outdoor target archery taken under cover and conducted at shorter ranges. Superficially it looks like that, but it is an over-simplification and archers subscribing to this theory create problems for themselves.

More indoor events take place today and more archers have the opportunity to shoot indoors where sympathetic managements of sports centres or owners of suitable halls have made this possible.

Indoor archery should be considered as a separate discipline from outdoor target archery and the archer should approach it as such.

The short distances (18m and 25m of the FITA indoor rounds) mean that the interval between the release and impact is very much shorter than outdoors. Archers who regard this indoor shooting as training for the coming outdoor season must be careful. They can become badly unstuck – this abbreviated time interval tends to speed up the archer's shooting sequence and kills the follow through unless the archer is aware of the situation and exerts firm self-discipline.

Target faces are smaller, 60cm at 25m and 40cm at 18m, and the degree of difficulty is increased. There is no room for sloppy shooting. Scores of 580 or better out of a possible 600 are now common at both distances in events such as the European Indoor Championships.

Posture is undeniably the major difference directly affecting the archer

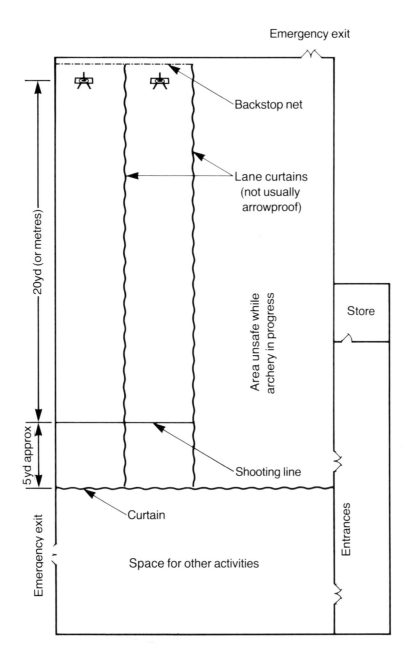

Typical community sports hall with archery facilities

coming in from the cold. A lot of archers make much of the so-called 'natural' position which, for the majority, is said to be when shooting at between 50 and 70m.

If the effectiveness of unit aiming is accepted wherein the archer pivots about the hips so that the relative positions of arms, shoulders and the upper part of the body remain unchanged at full draw, regardless of distance, then the concept of the 'natural' position becomes a fallacy.

When an archer says that he is more comfortable at one distance than at others it is often found that he leans his body away from the target as he draws his bow and then adjusts elevation by moving his bow arm. Thus there will be a distance at which the front arm will be more in line with the shoulders. Not only would this be more comfortable but shooting at that distance would be relatively more effective.

Indoors just as much as outdoors there should be a positive relationship between initial trajectory of the arrow and deviation of the upper part of the spine from the vertical. The target centre at 130cm above ground both indoors and out is therefore below eye level for most people. Outdoors this does not matter, for the initial trajectory will be elevated. With unit aiming, the upper part of the body will lean away from the target and the vertical through the centre of gravity of the upper body will be closer to the back foot.

Indoors at 25m the trajectory will be very nearly in a straight line, particularly with the more potent bows, and the arrow could start on its way on a slightly downward path, more noticeable if the archer is above average in height.

At 18m the depression will be greater. Here the archer should note that for the 18m indoor round the target faces may be set in two rows with centres at 160cm and 100cm above the floor. There will be a minute amount of elevation when shooting at the upper row and very marked depression of the shots at the lower row.

These indoor arrow trajectories have a direct bearing on the archer's posture. Depression, if the archer maintains his unit aiming as he should, takes the vertical through the centre of gravity of the upper body closer to the front foot. This is completely foreign to outdoor target archers and, repeated for so many successive arrows, is also foreign to field archers unused to this kind of repetition who have only to contend with random downhill shots. The outdoor target archer often says he dislikes indoor archery because of these depressed shots, while the same person will move over to field archery and take the downhill shots and the 'bunnies' in his stride, using unit aiming as if he knew no other way!

Apart from shelter from wind and rain, indoor archery has quite a different environment. The lighting level may be less intense and lacking in contrast compared with outdoors, while the noise level will be quite different. Sounds normally carried away on the wind become intrusive, especially the partially heard anecdote related behind the waiting line.

Do not expect all sports halls to be heated. Some are, but the archer should prepare for the worst. This goes for organisers and officials as well as the competitors. Thermal underwear and extra but easily removable layers of clothing make for comfort and a more relaxed performance.

Although straw target bosses are used at many indoor venues, Stramit or similar building board is a fairly common alternative. This makes it more difficult to withdraw the arrows and the arrow puller comes into its own.

Target faces are close together indoors and while archers shoot one at a time at each face they will find that they have less space on the shooting line and must take care not to disturb their neighbours. Space behind the waiting line is restricted, so good archers will be tidy archers, keeping clutter to a minimum and leaving room for fellow archers to get to and from the shooting line.

CHAPTER TWELVE

Youth, Disability and the Future

One of the best ways of developing archery as both sport and recreation is to attract, inspire and retain young people. Those who seek to do this have to be aware of the competition – the world is full of interesting alternatives, both active and passive and so archery must beat this competition.

Archery as a family activity offers the finest incentive to the junior members. When parents and children take part together and enjoy their shooting, it strengthens both club and family bonds. This helps to take the children through adolescence into maturity, opening their eyes to other things but ensuring at the same time that archery remains the major force.

Often the children experience archery before their parents through summer camps, adventure holidays, at school or sports centre.

Thus far archery is just for fun but some will find a natural competitive instinct and a natural ability to develop the skills for successful shooting. This is how many of today's champions have developed both in the United Kingdom and abroad.

Archery in summer camps
Here there can be a sausage machine approach; the admirable intention is to give the young people a taste of each of several activities which they might not encounter at home. The time is split up so that each group has only a few hours at archery.

The instructor must ensure that neither the children themselves nor any third party will stand into any kind of danger. The task is to get the children shooting as quickly and as safely as possible. Time is limited, the range short and the children want to shoot as many arrows as they can in the time.

Under such circumstances the formal target style is too complex for many youngsters. The side of face hand and string position as for bare bow shooting, using the point of the arrow instead of any kind of bow sight, is more readily understood and reasonable success can be achieved.

Those who want to find out more can always ask questions, while films and videos of archery will whet many appetites. Those who want more may be able to do so on return home – at least they can explore possible contacts in the neighbourhood or at school.

Equipment is limited and may be of poor standard (the despair of the instructors) and unsuitable specification, where the instructors have difficulty in matching draw weights and arrow lengths to their pupils. It may be years old, while the managements of some activity holidays have policies of borrowing to avoid transport costs and having tackle unused for eleven months of the year. There is scope for improvement here – with consumer pressure for better standards of management and instruction at summer camps comes a requirement for more acceptable equipment.

Archery in sports centres

As far as the younger participants are concerned, similar considerations apply here as in summer camps. They just want to shoot arrows – the development of skills and a sound approach to shooting form might just possibly come later.

There is better control over the minimum age for intake, though this minimum age is a subject for debate. The consensus is that, where no parental involvement exists, age eleven and upwards is a group more responsive to instruction and more in control of the body. Under that age time not shooting is boredom time – a distraction for the instructor who must keep an eye on those actually shooting.

The greatest attributes of the instructor are patience and perseverance. In the end he could take pride in knowing that some of his charges are capable of joining in club activity without causing embarrassment.

The instructor has more of a say about equipment and its purchase, while management will usually meet reasonable costs for maintenance and replacement, even when the instructor does the maintenance himself.

Archery in schools

Few schools have staff in the physical education department or on the academic side who are practising archers, let alone holders of archery coaching awards. Some may have visiting instructors but there are few archers and fewer still with coaching qualifications who are free during school hours. Today schools are a potential growth area for archery if only sufficient people with the right qualifications are on hand at the right time.

In the United Kingdom the GNAS offers a leader's certificate award for non-archers who have to develop archery in schools, youth clubs and sports centres and therefore require special training. There is a minimum training period of 20hr and the course, often arranged jointly by the local education authority and the local amateur coaching organisation, would include training in how to shoot so that trainees can give good account of themselves at about 20yd/m and can give effective demonstrations of and instruction in a simple basic technique.

On top of this they must be capable of basic maintenance of equipment –

141

straightening of arrows, replacing nocks, fletchings and piles, replacing serv-
ings and nocking points on bowstrings and, if possible, making bowstrings.
They must also be well versed in safety practices, including ground layout
and public liability cover.

Finally they must be aware of specialist sources of supply and of probable
costs – some of their pupils may want to buy personal items of equipment
and they will certainly need sound advice. In general it is best if they start
with accessories (tab, bracer, quiver and bow stand) and come to bows and
arrows later when they become more skilful.

Much more could be done at colleges of physical education to include
archery but this poses the question: who is to be responsible for the teaching
of archery at these colleges? This is something for the authorities to ponder
over.

If archery is to be brought into the curriculum, rather than as an out-of-
hours activity, thought must be given to the catchment years. Certainly it
has been successful when introduced at fourth and fifth year levels in
comprehensive schools with a carryover into the sixth form.

If there is only one archery teacher on hand there is a problem of cover for
absence. In no way can an untrained teacher stand in. It is sound policy to
have two or three staff members trained at the same time to supervise and
instruct. They can support each other in many ways, including the
maintenance of personal standards of performance in all their archery tasks.
Also to be borne in mind must be succession to take care of staff changes –
replacements must be forthcoming.

The nature of the activity and of its equipment calls for a great sense of
commitment on the part of teachers. This will be commitment of such a
degree that it ought at all times to override political and allied considerations
which undermine continuity.

Parental support

For children who have been bitten by the archery bug support from parents is
the most important factor. Such support takes various forms; purchase of
equipment, transporting the children to wherever they take part – sports
centre, club or tournament – and actual parental involvement in archery.

Of prime importance is actual parental involvement as archers. They know
exactly what is entailed, are able to encourage sensibly without excessive
expectations, can assist with care and maintenance of equipment and can give
coaching support in co-operation with the official coaches.

Next is transportation – tournaments for young archers are not very
common and often far from home. This means a lot of mileage with early
starts and late returns. Parents giving support in this way must do so freely
and without counting the cost – without harping on the subject. Parents
must never, never speak of all the other things they might rather have been

doing! Parental help in transporting school teams is also invaluable, but be aware of insurance problems and clear the question with insurers and school well in advance.

Much the same applies to the purchase of equipment – the guidance of the coach plus the approach advised in earlier chapters will transcend fashion and 'keeping up with the Joneses'. The most costly is rarely the best for a growing teenager still involved in learning and development.

Then there is parental 'support' where the child is expected to achieve instant success to erase the parents' own sense of childhood failure. It is painful to witness a parent nagging a child almost every time he or she comes off the shooting line – and yet it is not uncommon. Almost as bad is the gaggle of relatives behind the child's shooting position watching every shot through binoculars, turning a pleasurable outdoor exercise into a matter of life and death. This does no good to the sport because it kills enthusiasm and turns the child against the very thing he set out to enjoy.

If parents have nothing to do once they have transported their offspring to a tournament, let them report to the organisers – there is plenty to be done by way of scoring, serving refreshments or providing back-up for the work party.

Organisations and incentives

In the United Kingdom the GNAS makes special provision for junior archery in its various disciplines and operates its own junior award scheme where points are awarded for gaining AAS achievement badges (see below), improving GNAS classification or handicap rating, by competing, breaking records and being selected for teams or training squads. The club involvement is the forcing house for this scheme and club encouragement is vital for its success. Inaugurated in 1981, it covers target archery only but ways and means of extending the scheme to field archery are now under consideration.

For British schools the Association for Archery in Schools (AAS) has its achievement badge scheme based substantially on the number of arrows which can be shot in a limited time. AAS badges can be gained where shooting GNAS rounds is out of the question. Scores are graded by age and sex to encourage maximum participation.

The AAS organises its own tournaments and postal leagues, with sympathetic understanding of what is possible in schools. In these events there are classes for simple bows (one piece solid fibreglass bows), recurves and compounds with subdivisions by age and sex.

There is one further award to which young people can aspire in the United Kingdom and that is the Duke of Edinburgh Award with bronze, silver and gold levels of achievement. The GNAS has set the standards to provide the challenge to those encountering archery for the first time in the hope that they will be attracted, inspired and continue in the sport long after they have gained their awards.

Disability

Mention archery for the disabled and one immediately thinks of people in wheelchairs. This is only one form of disability. Disability takes many forms; for example, those with partial or totally impaired hearing have no outward and visible signs of their disability and yet it cuts them off from society just as much as being confined to a wheelchair and viewing the world from waist level. There are many other areas of handicap, among them amputees, sufferers from cerebral palsy, multiple sclerosis and haemophilia, as well as those with impaired vision.

Archery can be made available to all of these and even to some with mental disability. Where disability limits performance, archery as one of the activities of the local Sports Association for Disabled serves to broaden experience, but there are those who can perform at least as well as many able-bodied archers in spite of their handicap – it is great when they can join the wider community of archers.

The ideal approach is to issue a challenge – to find out what people can do if only they are given the chance. The things they cannot do are self-evident but with the right kind of help from dedicated able-bodied volunteers they can achieve wonders. There are many engineering aids that can support or take the place of damaged arms so that the bow can be aligned positively or the string released effectively while a notable development of recent years is the tactile sight for blind archers.

In the United Kingdom the GNAS not only makes provision for affiliation at little or no cost for archery clubs catering solely for disabled persons but also has its own liaison officer for the disabled. His function is to co-ordinate information on aids and facilities for disabled archers and to act as a focus for advice and assistance. The British Paraplegic Archery Association is an affiliated society of the GNAS and so caters for the special needs of those confined to wheelchairs through illness or accident.

The best way of finding out just what the disabled can do to respond to the challenge of archery is to work with the local Sports Association for Disabled. The main task is to achieve as much self-sufficiency as individual handicaps will allow, assisting with coaching, equipment maintenance and especially in doing those jobs that only the able bodied can do – setting up and unrigging targets, preparing equipment for use and stowing it away after an archery session.

Often overlooked is another aspect. Disabilities isolate the handicapped from the community. Archery is the one sporting activity where the disabled can take their place on the shooting line with able-bodied archers and compete on equal terms.

Devices like this enable amputees to enjoy the sport of archery

Positive location of the hand makes it possible for the blind or partially sighted to shoot with some degree of accuracy

Coaching here lies very often in guiding the archer towards shooting even just one arrow by whatever means. The achievement will be the shooting of that arrow, regardless of how far it goes or where it lands, and if it should hit a target that will be a bonus. If the archer has the will, it is up to the coach to help find a way.

Archery tomorrow

Events can overturn any prediction of what the future might hold. New materials and new designs to accommodate them are always possible.

Changes in attitudes, pressures from commerce or the media have affected other sports so archery cannot claim exemption. Already FITA's introduction of the Finals Round for major international contest shows a reaction to the need, real or imagined, to add excitement to an otherwise comparatively staid event. Television viewers seem incapable of watching unless there is continual action – or so the medium's managers would have the world believe. There is a parallel between this falsified air of excitement and the Romans throwing more and yet more Christians to the lions.

Watching is a passive activity. Participation is the name of the game, but interest generated by television may change the attitudes of both private and public bodies and their supporters towards providing greater and easier access to land for archery, and may even transform watchers into archers.

Reports from the 1987 European Indoor Championships in Paris show that more than 6,000 spectators attended on the final day. A giant video screen and many cameras allowed spectators to see close-ups of competitors and slow motion pictures of shooting form. Electronic score indicators kept everybody informed while there was a full hour of television coverage for a much wider audience. The French succeeded in making a spectacle of the event without changing the format, proof that it can be done.

Now FITA has its eye on developing nations and on junior archers. Both groups are 'underprivileged' in terms of material and financial resources. To meet their special needs FITA has now (October 1987) published Appendix 14 to its Constitution and Rules which defines the Standard Bow and accessories, regulates its use in competition and provides for appropriate awards. This Standard Bow concept has already been welcomed by many coaches and administrators and, while some archers may scorn the idea, there is much to be said in its favour as a means of developing and expanding the sport around the world. It will be in the interests of both manufacturers and distributors to wholeheartedly support this development.

Expansion in archery is like milk in a bottle with cream rising to the top. There will be neither the quantity nor the quality of cream if there is little underneath. Competitive pressure among those entering the sport will ultimately challenge the champions into achieving greater success. Quantity must come before quality can fully develop, and expansion of the sport will in due time enhance competition at the highest levels.

Another change for the better would be the divergence of sporting activity within the universities, teacher training colleges and colleges of physical education. The concentration on the 'traditional' cricket, association and rugby football, and excessive concentration on sports science to the detriment of participation at beginner and recreational levels need urgent rethinking towards the end of a century that has seen a dramatic increase in mobility and available leisure time in many countries. If any sporting activity is 'traditional' then surely in the United Kingdom, if nowhere else, archery should head the list.

Finance is a headache in any voluntary organisation. In sports like archery three sources of funding are available. First comes that from the archers themselves: if they want rules of the game, a coaching scheme, people to hold the sport together and people to organise the competitions then they must put up the money to make these things possible. A second source is sponsorship: commercial undertakings will only inject funds if some return is likely – this means open display of name, emblem or product where spectators and viewers can see them; this is why television coverage is seen to be so important a goal. The third possible source is from central or local government. Understandably there will be strings attached. For minority sports where the interest is in participation and spectators are rare there is no gate money to augment subscription income, so grant aid is not to be turned away in spite of the conditions that come with it.

Government attitudes change with the political and economic climate and grant aid can change or cease without notice. A guaranteed five or ten year plan would enable a sporting governing body to plan ahead with greater efficiency and to invest in development projects in the knowledge that they would have time to be tested and come to fruition. Today far too much grant aid is on a hand-to-mouth basis because no such guarantees exist in grant aid policy.

It is said that too much money is spent on international involvement and competition. However, those who give the aid also specify where it should be spent and international contest figures high on the list.

In recent years there has been a tendency for society to emphasise its rights and overlook its responsibilities. It is impossible to have one without the other. One man's right is another's responsibility.

Development of archery is the responsibility of all participants – it cannot be delegated, so for the wellbeing of archery tomorrow there has to be a concerted effort by the archers of today. If this means the sacrifice of a tithe of shooting time in order to give more time to coaching, organising or administration, or in tackling those who have the power to support by cash, by places for shooting or in kind, then so be it. Make that sacrifice and archery both today and tomorrow can only benefit.

Glossary

AAS Association for Archery in Schools; UK body that promotes archery as a school activity, encouraging this through its achievement badge scheme and tournaments for young people

AIM To align body and bow with target using bow sight or other method for elevation and lateral adjustment so that arrows strike where intended

AMO Archery Manufacturers Organisation, group of manufacturers in USA who work together to set standards of performance, dimensions and interchangeability

ANCHOR *see* Reference Point

ANIMAL ROUNDS Field archery rounds using pictures of animals as target faces

ARROW PLATE Vertical material to which arrow rest is attached; insert of hard material in side of long bow to resist wear from arrow

ARROW REST Attachment on side of bow on which the arrow rests before release, designed to minimise deflection of arrow

BACK ARM Arm farther from target, often 'drawing arm' or 'string arm'

BACK (OF BOW) Side of bow farther from string

BARE BOW Style of shooting mainly in field archery. Bows used are bare of attachments

BELLY (OF BOW) Side of bow nearer to string, also 'front' or 'face'

BOW SIGHT Attachment on bow to assist aiming

BRACE To bend bow so that string fits into and is stretched between nocks at each end

BRACER Item strapped to bow arm to keep clothing from path of string on release, also protects arm if struck by string

BRACING HEIGHT Perpendicular distance from bow string to point on bow, usually to throat of handle or to back of bow in line with nocking point

BULLET PILE *see* Pile

BUNNY Colloquial term for 15cm target faces in FITA field archery, derived from small faces in animal rounds

BUSH Threaded insert or hole in handle of bow into which stabilisers, pressure buttons and sight attachments may be fitted

148

BUTT, BUTTRESS *see* Target Boss

CLOUT SHOOTING Form of archery contest at almost twice maximum target archery distance with flag (clout) as aiming mark

COME DOWN! Instruction from coach to pupil to stop pupil from completing shot

COMPOSITE BOW *see* Recurve Bow

COMPOUND BOW Bow that gives mechanical advantage by means of cams or pulleys

CRESTING Coloured bands just forward of the fletching on an arrow which distinguish one archer's arrows from another's

DACRON Polyester fibre for making bowstrings, preferred for beginners', club and compound bows, kinder to bows of older designs

DEPRESSION Inclination of body towards target to give lower arrow trajectory

DRAWING HAND Hand that holds and releases string

DRAW WEIGHT Force required to draw a bow to exactly accommodate an arrow of given length, eg 40lb at 28in. Draw weights always quoted in pounds and arrow lengths in inches. Metric equivalents rarely given.

ELEVATION Inclination of body away from target to give higher arrow trajectory

END Set number of arrows shot by each archer before going to targets to score

FAST! Traditional call for immediate halt to all shooting because of unexpected hazard, contraction from 'Hold fast!'

FIBREGLASS BOW Simple one-piece bow made entirely of fibreglass. Both straight and recurved types are used

FIELD ARCHERY Archery in varied terrain, shooting at different distances at targets of different sizes, moving from target to target in sequence

FIELD CAPTAIN Person responsible for controlling shooting in club or at tournament. Known as Director of Shooting in FITA context

FITA Fédération Internationale de Tir à l'Arc, international governing body for archery affiliated to International Olympic Committee

FLETCHING Craft of fitting feather or plastics vanes to arrows

FLETCHINGS Vanes fitted to arrows to give stability in flight

FOLLOW THROUGH Maintenance of line of sight and arm positions as they end up after the release

FOOT MARKERS Small pegs or similar items placed in ground to indicate location of archer's feet when shooting

FREE STYLE Method of shooting with bow sight used in both field and target archery

FRONT ARM Arm nearer target, alternatively bow arm

GAP Vertical space seen by archer between target and arrow point, method of aiming in bare bow style

GNAS Grand National Archery Society, national governing body for archery in United Kingdom, affiliated to FITA and British Olympic Committee

GRIP Manufacturers' term for part of bow held by archer when shooting; preferred term is 'handle'

HANDICAP TABLES Tables used by target archers in United Kingdom to derive handicaps for competition and to equate performance from scores in different rounds

KEVLAR Manmade fibre used for making bowstrings, has little elasticity hence liked by keenly competitive archers but has relatively short life

KISSER Attachment on bow string used by some archers to obtain secondary reference point at mouth

LIMBS Working parts of a bow in which energy is stored when bow is drawn

LINE OF SIGHT Straight line between aiming eye and chosen mark or target centre

LONG BOW Traditional weapon of Medieval and Tudor England and of 19th- and early 20th-century sporting archers, typically about 6ft (1.8m) long with deep D-shaped cross-section

MASTER BOWMAN GNAS classification of archer indicating high level of performance

METAL DETECTOR Electronic instrument used to detect buried metal, used in archery to find arrows that have missed target

NOCK 1 Slot in end of arrow that fits onto string

2 Grooves at each end of bow in which loops of bowstring are placed to brace bow ready for shooting

3 Act of fitting arrow to bowstring

NOCKING POINT Point on bowstring indicating by means of thread, metal or plastics locators exact position of arrow for repetition of shot

ONE-PIECE BOW Bow where handle and limbs are assembled as single indivisible unit

PILE Point of competition arrow, now usually with ogival (bullet) rather than angular (conical) profile

PRESSURE BUTTON Spring loaded device to help arrow leave bow cleanly, adjusted when tuning bow

QUIVER Container from which arrows can easily be taken, worn on belt or across shoulders

RECURVE BOW Bow complying with current FITA definition, also known as composite bow from laminated construction of its limbs. Can be one-piece or take-down.

REFERENCE POINT Point on archer's face to which string is brought for every shot, also point of contact of drawing hand with face, commonly called 'anchor' or 'anchor point'

RELEASE 1 Act of letting string leave fingers, also known as 'loose'

2 Mechanical device used to draw and release string by
'unlimited' class compound archers and by some disabled
archers

ROUND Basis for competition and records in given form of archery, a
combination of numbers of arrows, distances and target sizes, eg FITA
Outdoor Target Round, Hereford Round, FITA Hunters Round

SERVING Thread wrapped round bowstring at loops and in centre to
protect strands from wear

SHAFT Main part of arrow, excluding pile, nock and fletchings, also
alternative term for complete arrow

SHELF Horizontal projection at bottom of sight window formerly used as
arrow rest

SHIRT GUARD Triangular piece of leather or plastics worn on chest to
keep clothing clear of bowstring on release, also known as chest guard

SHOOTING LINE Line on target archery range from which all archers
shoot

SIGHT WINDOW Cut out part in handle section of bow enabling both
line of sight and axis of arrow to lie close to, on or inside of centre line of bow

SLING Device to keep bow from falling from open hand after release

STABILISER Weight attached to handle section of bow to increase mass
and slow down movement in hand on release, usually mounted on rod at
distance from bow to shift centre of gravity

STANDARD BOW Bow specified by FITA for use by archers and/or
nations with limited resources. (Standard Round devised for this bow)

TAB Shaped piece of leather or substitute worn on fingers of drawing hand
to allow smooth consistent release, often fitted with platform for use with
side of face reference point

TAKE-DOWN BOW Bow with limbs made separately and attached to
handle with bolts or other means

TARGET ARCHERY Archery discipline taking place on flat open field
with common shooting line and targets at distances to suit men, women and
juniors

TARGET BOSS Circular compressed straw mat resistant to arrow
penetration to which target face is fixed. Stramit building board or other
materials also used to make square butt or buttress for same purpose.

TFC Torque flight compensator; adjustable flexible coupling fitted between
stabiliser rod and handle of bow to damp down vibrations, not used with
long rods

UNIT AIMING Head, shoulders, arms and upper part of body moved as
single unit to give necessary elevation, depression or traversing for shot

ZEN Japanese religious or mystical approach expressed through traditional
crafts or martial arts.

Suggested further reading

Most books listed below can be borrowed through local public libraries or, if still in print, purchased from larger specialist archery retailers.

ASCHAM, Roger. *Toxophilus* (Reprint by Manchester University [UK], 1985); the first book on archery in the English language.

ELMER, R. P. *Target Archery* (Hutchinson [UK] 1952); a classic, reviewing the state of the art up to the time of World War II.

HADAS, L. *Champions* (LFH Film Productions [USA], 1980); lavishly illustrated photographic record of leading performers in archery, useful for analytical study.

HEATH, E. G. *Archery – A Military History* (Osprey [UK], 1980); a wide ranging study by an archery historian, which includes an account of what it feels like to be hit by an arrow, albeit a target arrow and not a broadhead.

HENDERSON, A. *Understanding Winning Archery* (Target Communications Corporation [USA] 1983); commonsense approach to competitive archery and the problems that beset too many archers.

HERRIGEL, E. *Zen in the Art of Archery* (Routledge & Kegan Paul [UK], 1956); here archery is subsidiary to a study of Zen Buddhism but nevertheless an interesting approach.

HOLDEN, J. *Shooting Straight* (Crowood Press [UK], 1987); an in-depth study of currently available types of equipment and accessories including hunting tackle and compound bows.

LOISELLE, E. *How to Doctor your own Compound bow*

MATTHEWS, R. *Bow Tuning* (Les Howis [Marksman] Bows Ltd [UK], 1984); a step by step guide to setting up a recurve bow and then tuning it for optimum performance.

MATTHEWS, R. & HOLDEN, J. *Archery in Earnest* (Crowood Press [UK], 1985); a considered examination of shooting form with a section on equipment and tuning.

PETERSON, Blair A. *Behind the Bow* (Galant Publishing Co [USA], 1977); recommended for those who shoot compound bows.

SMITH, M. F. *Archery* (Ward Locke [UK], 1978); a basic approach, following coaching theory of the time.

STAMP, D. G. *The Challenge of Archery* (A. & C. Black [UK], 1971); another basic approach in some detail, which has not aged appreciably.

STAMP, D. G. *Field Archery* (A. & C. Black [UK], 1979); an expert's overview of this fascinating branch of the sport, including chapters on course layout and the making and maintenance of equipment.

MANUALS

Federation of Canadian Archers, *Instructor's Manual*

Federation of Canadian Archers, *Coaches' Manual* (various levels)

National Archery Association of USA, *Instructor's Manual*

Grand National Archery Society, *Coaches' Manual*

PERIODICALS (available only from the publishers or from specialist archery retailers)

Canada:	*The Canadian Archer*
United Kingdom:	*The British Archer* (Bi-monthly)
	The Glade (Quarterly)
United States of America:	*Archery World*
	Bow and Arrow
	US Archer Magazine

RULES OF SHOOTING

Fédération Internationale de Tir à l'Arc: *Constitution and Rules*

Grand National Archery Society: *Rules of Shooting*

Many nations have their own domestic rules which, while broadly following FITA, preserve local traditions and meet local conditions.

Acknowledgements

To *The British Archer* magazine for permission to include the photograph of Roy Mundon.

Appendix 1

Units of measurement

In archery today certain conventions over dimensions and the units in which they are quoted are commonly accepted and have been adhered to in this book.

The linear dimensions of bows and arrows are given by manufacturers and distributors in inches and fractions of an inch. Draw weights of bows are given in pounds while the mass of an arrow or of its pile would be in grains.

Traditional British rounds like the York and Hereford and those like the American, which have developed in the United States, all have their distances specified in yards.

In the same way the distances shot in FITA competitions, dimensions of target faces and their respective tolerances are all in metric units.

There are no exact equivalents in round figures of one system in the other which can be easily remembered. It would be meaningless to quote equivalents in the main text because the archers themselves do not use them. However some readers may insist on translating from one system to the other and for them the following conversion factors will be helpful:

1in = 25.4mm	1cm = 0.3937in
⅛in = 3.18mm	1mm = 0.03937in
1yd = 0.914m	1m = 39.37in or 1.0936yd

1lb = 0.4536kg
1 grain = 64.8mg

Appendix 2

Suggested equipment specifications for new archers (a) using pooled equipment and (b) making their first purchases

Description of archer	Probable draw length (inches)	For initial training (first lessons at 10–15yd/m)			For continuation training at 20–25yd/m			For first purchases, shooting at intermediate distances only		
		Male	Female	Bow length	Male	Female	Bow length	Male	Female	Bow length
Child, small teenage	24 or less	a	a	m, q	e	e	m, q	d	d	v
Mid teenage, small woman	24 to 26	b	b	n, r	e	e	n, r	g	f	w
Late teenage, small man, average woman	25 to 27	c	c	o, s	d	d	p, s	g	f	x
Late teenage (tall), average man, tall woman	26 to 28	c	c	p, t	f	d	p, t	h	f	y
Late teenage (tallest), tall man	27 to 31 or more	d	—	p, u	g	—	p, u	h	—	u

These suggested specifications should help to make the best use of existing items and avoid the use of grossly unsuitable equipment. They are for guidance only and may have to be varied to suit some individuals.

Key to Appendix 2

Draw weights
a   15lb at 24in
b   15lb at 26in
c   15 to 20lb at 28in
d   20 to 25lb at 30in
e   15 to 25lb at 24in
f   25 to 30lb at 30in
g   25 to 35lb at 30in
h   30 to 35lb at 30in

Bow lengths, fibreglass types
m   48 to 54in
n   54 to 56in
o   54 to 60in
p   60in (longest currently available in UK)

Bow lengths, recurve types
q   48 to 54in
r   62 to 64in
s   62 to 66in
t   64 to 68in
u   68 to 72in
v   54in
w   62in
x   64in
y   66 to 70in

Appendix 3

One thing at a time
or, A simple order of shooting with the bow
A typical reminder of the order of shooting an arrow given out at a sports centre.

Take your place on the shooting line with your bow and arrows

Get your feet in the right position before you do anything else – and then keep your feet still until you have shot all your arrows

Put your arrows down almost touching your toes so that you only need to bend down to pick them up – bending at the knees and keeping the body upright is the best way (and good exercise, too)

Check your hold of the bow and bring the bow in front of you so that it is like a work surface. Keep that same hold until you have shot all your arrows.

With the other hand lay an arrow on the bow and guide its nock onto the bowstring

Place the fingers on the string – not too little, not too much but just right

Pause

Stand upright, breathe in deeply and breathe out

Pause

Turn your head to the target and fix your gaze on the place you want to hit (the centre spot or the gold). Keep your attention on this mark until your arrow has landed.

Pause

Raise the bow until the sight pin is on the line between your eye and the mark

Both arms must be at or slightly above shoulder level

Draw the bow, pressing the bow towards the target with the front arm and pushing away from the target with the elbow of the back arm to bring the bowstring to touch your face

The bowstring must stay touching your face until you let go

Keep pressing and pushing back as you let your fingers straighten so that as you loose the arrow your hands move apart naturally

Keep your hands and arms up until the arrow has hit the target

Bring your hands down to your sides

Pause

Repeat exactly the same actions for every arrow you shoot.

There is a lot more to archery than this and your coach or instructor will help you to find this out. Get the order of shooting right and it will help your instructor to help you.

Remember that archery is marksmanship using the bow and arrow.

Everything that you do must be exact and under control.

Good shooting!

Appendix 4

International and national governing bodies for archery

(For this list only the English speaking nations have been selected from the 70 currently listed in the FITA Directory.)

Fédération Internationale de Tir à l'Arc, FITA Executive Bureau, Via Cerva 30, 20122, Milan, Italy

Archery Association of Australia, 7 Cherry Street, Glen Waverley, Victoria, Australia

Federation of Canadian Archers, Inc, c/o The Honor System, 90 Cavehill Crescent, Scarborough, Ontario, M1R 1M1, Canada

The Grand National Archery Society, 7th Street, National Agricultural Centre, Stoneleigh, Kenilworth, Warwickshire, CV8 2LG, England

Irish National Archery Federation, 22 Oaklawn Estate, Leixlip, Co Kildare, Ireland

New Zealand Archery Association, PO Box 24–091, Christchurch, New Zealand

South African National Archery Association, PO Box 120, Constantia 7848, Cape Town, Republic of South Africa

National Archery Association of the United States, 1750 East Boulder Street, Colorado Springs, CO 80909, USA

Index